The Practical Executive and Workforce Diversity

WILLIAM SONNENSCHEIN

Series Editor, Arthur H. Bell, Ph.D.

Printed on recyclable paper

NTC Business Books
a division of *NTC Publishing Group* • Lincolnwood, Illinois USA

Library of Congress Cataloging-in-Publication Data

Sonnenschein, William.
   The practical executive and workforce diversity / by William
Sonnenschein.
      p.   cm.
   Includes bibliographical references and index.
   ISBN 0-8442-2981-4 (alk. paper)
   1. Diversity in the workplace—Management. 2. Multiculturalism
—Management. 3. Personnel management. I. Title.
HF5549.5.M5S66   1997
658.3'041—dc20   96-35853
                                                                CIP

Published by NTC Business Books, a division of NTC Publishing Group
4255 West Touhy Avenue
Lincolnwood (Chicago), Illinois 60646-1975, U.S.A.
© 1997 by NTC Publishing Group. All rights reserved.
No part of this book may be reproduced, stored in a retrieval system,
or transmitted in any form or by any means,
electronic, mechanical, photocopying, recording or otherwise,
without the prior permission of NTC Publishing Group.
Manufactured in the United States of America.

6 7 8 9 0 VP 9 8 7 6 5 4 3 2 1

Contents

Preface

Diversity training has become a virtual industry in the 1990s. Approximately two-thirds of American companies offered some form of diversity training in 1995, up from 47 percent in 1993 and 40 percent in 1992.

And no wonder. Department of Labor predictions for Workforce 2000 depict a heterogeneous group of employees, with significant representation of women, racial and ethnic minorities, people with disabilities, and others. In fact, of the 21 million new jobs expected to open through the year 2005, fully 85 percent are projected to be filled by women and minorities.

At the same time, business opportunities both within the United States and throughout the world require that American workers are adept in languages, aware of cultural differences, and savvy to regional and global markets.

Managers at all levels therefore have powerful motives to learn new management insights and skills for new workforce realities. That's the entrance cue for William Sonnenschein's book.

Here Sonnenschein teaches all levels of management—not just how to survive an increasingly diverse employee base, but how to make the most of it—even celebrate it. Drawing from his many years as a diversity consultant for major companies and organizations, he teaches the techniques *that work* in managing employees from diverse backgrounds and experiences.

That diversity, Sonnenschein insists, includes each of us. White males in particular are not exempt from Sonnenschein's analysis; they do not stand apart from the new wave of employees but are themselves part of the diversity that must be managed effectively.

No manager has the luxury of ignoring the diversity issue in the final years of the 1990s and beyond. In the words of Bill Stone, diversity trainer for Chevron, "We can either let diversity work against us or turn it into an asset."

Sonnenschein here presents the specific tools—and a complete set it is indeed—that business leaders at all levels will need for managing diversity as an asset. These tools, tested in practice, are ready to come out of the box for use on the job.

Arthur H. Bell
McLaren School of Business
University of San Francisco
January, 1996

Acknowledgments

Many people gave their time, energy, and encouragement during the process of writing this book.

First and foremost, thank you Ericka Lutz. Most writers rightly thank their families for the incredible amount of tolerance and support they give those who write and live with them. My partner in marriage, though, is special. She is a professional writer and editor who literally edited this book. Her love and dedication to this project made it all possible.

Special thanks to Karen Lovaas. Karen was my partner in diversity consulting for several years, and some of the material in this book grew out of that partnership.

Thank you Rick Isaacson for always being there for me, Terry Pearce for constantly keeping on me to give my best and get it done, Karla Lutz and Arthur Lutz, Ralph Manak, Barry Eckhouse, Bob Jemerson, my students at the Haas School of Business, University of California, Berkeley. Thanks to Anna Mindess for invaluable information about the deaf. Special thanks to Andy Shogan, Dean of Instruction at the Haas School of Business, for believing in the Humanities approach to Business Communication.

To my children, Aaron, Rachel, and Annie, for support and love.

And thank you Art Bell, whose faith and belief in me made this book a reality.

Introduction

This book is a tool kit for making the potential benefits of diversity a reality in your workplace. While the primary audience for this book is business executives, and many of the tools included are for people in leadership positions, anyone can use it. Leadership skills are not positional; they are for everyone at all levels of the organizational chart. The skills in this book will help you and your organization reap the benefits of diversity.

Communication is key to being an effective executive in today's diverse workplace. This book will help you:

- Translate the potential benefits of diversity into tangible, productive workplace gains.
- Enhance your flexibility in diverse communication situations.
- Improve your cross-group speaking and listening skills.
- Recognize and suspend your assumptions and stereotypes.
- Gain respect for and appreciation of differences.
- Contribute to a supportive, nondiscriminatory, and productive work environment.

The communication goals of executives as leaders in their organizations include:

- Improving working relationships in their organizations, based on mutual respect and an increased knowledge of multicultural issues.

- Reducing interpersonal conflict among employees as understanding and respect grows.

- Increasing productivity as more employee effort goes to task performance, and less time and energy goes to managing interpersonal and intercultural conflicts.

- Creating a greater commitment to a shared organizational vision among diverse employees at all levels and in all functions.

- Stimulating more creativity, innovation, and flexibility as all employees participate more fully in decision-making and problem-solving.

Gaining the benefits of diversity is not an easy task. The organizational change created by diversity is significant, but it is vital for executives to create workplace environments in which employees from different backgrounds can develop awareness, attitudes, and communication skills that will enable them to work together more productively. The more executives take on leadership roles in these areas, the stronger their organizations will be.

Some diversity books concentrate on creating mechanisms to manage diversity. Others focus on understanding individual cultures or recognizing cultural patterns. Some use a psychological approach. This book emphasizes leadership and communication skills that will improve understanding, responsibility, and empowerment and thereby increase the welfare and productivity of organizations.

ORGANIZATION

This book covers each step you need to take to prosper in a diverse workplace. To fully understand the diversity skills you need, you must know what diversity is, its benefits and challenges, and the skills an effective executive and leader needs. This information is in Chapter One.

You also need to fully understand the issues diversity creates, both to know how best to lead a diverse workforce and to be aware of situations in the workplace that need attention. Chapter Two examines societal diversity issues as well as issues specific to the workplace.

Both diversity and leadership skills begin by understanding what we as individuals bring to the workplace and how we communicate who we are. Chapter Three offers tools for increasing self-awareness, including understanding your cultural identity, values, and perceptions.

The next communication skill is understanding others. Chapter Four presents active listening and empathy, the skills needed to understand people who are different from you.

Chapter Five offers tools for communicating *to* people from diverse backgrounds, including the use of inclusive language, proactive listening, and other communication techniques.

The final five chapters offer tools executives need to communicate as leaders in a diverse workplace.

The knowledge of how to develop and maintain good teams is one of the most important skills a leader needs in today's organizational world. Chapter Six looks at the skills needed to build teams and offers a unique tool for developing high-performance teams made up of members from diverse backgrounds.

Diversity, by its very nature, creates conflict, which means that it creates problems. But conflict also creates many benefits. Chapter Seven explores the notion of managing conflict so it is beneficial rather than destructive.

Chapter Eight looks at perhaps the most established leadership communication skill: how leaders use language to create cooperation, to inspire, motivate, and persuade, and to create realities and the fulfillment of visions.

As organizations change, though, executives must be skillful in guiding those changes. Chapter Nine looks at cultural change in organizations and offers tools to lead those changes.

Finally, Chapter Ten offers tools for creating an open environment and helping everyone in your organization gain the diversity communication skills needed to make your differences produce positive outcomes. These skills include modeling, mentoring, and coaching.

1

Defining Diversity

The person who figures out how to harness the collective genius of the people in his or her organization is going to blow the competition away.

Walter Wriston
former Citibank CEO[1]

During the last ten years, every level of CG Department Stores has seen an increase in the number of women and people of color. The mail room, once totally male, is now 40 percent female. Mid-management, formerly almost entirely white, now includes 20 percent people of color. Diversity has also had an impact on upper management. An African American man became Comptroller and Senior Vice-President three years ago.

WORKPLACE DIVERSITY

The demographics of the workplace are changing and will continue to change rapidly. Almost every organization in the United States looks different—both in terms of who's employed and the positions they hold—than it did ten years ago.

The Hudson Institute study, Workforce 2000, projects that between 1988 and 2000 only 15 percent of the people entering the workforce will be American-born white males. In 1987, this figure stood at 48 percent. In the year 2000, two-thirds of new workers will be women. The rate of people of color joining the workforce will be much greater than the rate of whites. Many of these new entrants will not speak English. The workforce will also be older.

Workforce diversity is not a matter for debate. It's a fact. It presents one of the greatest challenges facing today's organizations, and only through hard work and committed leadership can the potential for benefit be realized. Yet where will the leadership come from? How many leaders do we need? What skills must they have? This book provides answers to these questions.

What Is Diversity?

If you push it far enough, each of us is a distinct individual, different from everyone else in the universe. That is certainly true, but it is not the context within which diversity is operating in the workplace. Diversity as it is discussed here is the result of a broad range of complex social, political, economic, and other forces that have put in close proximity people who have vastly different orientations, frames of reference, backgrounds, and perspectives.

This book will concentrate on differences of race, culture, gender, sexual orientation, age, and physical abilities. These differences can unleash forces that can tear an organization apart or, by drawing from the potential strengths inherent in these differences, make a powerful, dynamic organization.

Diversity's Challenges

Diversity, though, means challenge. Racism, sexism, ageism, and homophobia disrupt the workplace, prevent teams from accomplishing their goals, and keep organizations from achieving their missions. Even simple misunderstandings caused by cultural and other differences in behavior, work attitudes, and communication styles disrupt the workplace. Executives need to be aware of the challenges of diversity. Only with that awareness can they rise to the challenges and reap the benefits of diversity.

Diversity's Benefits

The substantial differences among the members of today's workforce can mean substantial benefits for today's organizations—if leaders will work to realize those benefits. Diversity means differences, and differences create challenges; but differences also open avenues of opportunities never before imagined. Diversity enables a wide range of views to be present in an organization, including new, potentially more effective ways of doing things.

Numerous studies have documented the benefits. Companies that have successfully developed a diverse workforce have saved millions of dollars on turnover costs, improved product quality, and produced twice the rate of return on investment as those which did not use their diversity as well.[2]

3M is an organization dedicated to valuing the diversity of its workforce. Richard Lidstad, Vice President of Human Resources, says that respect is the key to embracing diversity. He tells the story of coming to 3M many years ago, during an era when male executives always wore business suits. Much to his surprise, a man in his laboratory wore sport shirts, Hush Puppies, and had a scraggly beard. The man turned out to be one of the company's top inventors, a holder of 13 patents. People had so much respect for him and for what he had accomplished that they learned to ignore how he dressed. Lidstad uses that story to stress the importance of doing more than tolerating differences. To be a successful executive, he says, you need to embrace differences in people, their cultures, their different ways of behaving, in the world.[3]

IBM believes the diversity of its workforce means understanding and appealing to its customer base. As the company has downsized, it has assigned a special workforce diversity staff to assure that its workplace diversity remains intact. As IBM chief Louis V. Gerstner says, "Our marketplace is made up of all races, religions, and sexual orientations, and therefore it is vital to our success that our workforce also be diverse." The organization's Director of Workplace Diversity adds, "We think it is important for our customers to look inside and see people like them. If they can't, it seems to me the prospect of them becoming our staying customers declines."[4]

Organizational Challenges

One of the biggest challenges of diversity is how it affects the management of organizations. Some of the specific organizational challenges that diversity creates are:

- Management complexity: A homogenous organization has less surface conflict. There is no need to accommodate to different ways of acting and communicating.

- Fairness: It is necessary to define "fairness" and to create mechanisms to ensure that every individual is treated equitably.

- Individual differences vs. unanimity: Employees need to make a conscious effort to learn to work with people with different styles, to understand new perspectives, and to adjust to disparate attitudes.

- Identity and loyalty: It becomes necessary to create a sense of community among people who, at the outset, may wonder if they can trust one another.

Turning many of these challenges into benefits is possible. Finding new approaches to doing tasks, for instance, leads to innovation. Clear-thinking executives with sound diversity skills can find the ways to make diversity work.

LEADERSHIP

Perhaps the most important diversity skills are leadership skills. There are many definitions of leadership and many leadership styles, but it might be summed up by what it is (style) and what it does (role or function).

Leadership Styles

One view breaks leadership down to four different styles:

- A *visionary* leader sees a future, sets goals, and communicates a shared vision.
- A *motivational* leader communicates in a way that inspires others to act.
- An *archetypal* leader models ways of doing things, or acts in a way he or she wishes others to act.
- A *facilitator* assures that everyone is heard and that everyone shares in the responsibilities and outcomes of organizational missions.

Peter Senge sees a leader as someone who understands the different needs of an organization, and plays a variety of roles:[5]

The leader as *designer* designs his or her organization by establishing the organization's core values and purpose, and by communicating its vision. The leader creates policies, strategies, and systems based on those concepts.

The leader as *teacher* tells "stories" that describe the truth about the organization, and fills others with a sense of purpose. The leader is a coach, a guide, a facilitator, and helps others in the organization generate ideas for the future rather than merely react or respond to outside stimuli.

The leader as *steward* is the "keeper" of the organization's vision. The leader tests ideas, listens to others, and changes his or her personal vision as he or she talks with others. His or her personal vision is not as important as the vision of the organization. The leader unifies all people and creates a shared vision.

What Leadership Does

Effective leaders, no matter style, help create awareness of both the issues of diversity and of the ways to communicate in a diverse workplace. To do this, they must be aware of the issues, be self-aware, and be open to different styles of communication. By possessing these characteristics and skills, the effective leader understands how to motivate each unique individual. A manager gets the most out of his or her workforce, and a leader gets even more.

COMMUNICATION

Leadership requires excellent communication skills. Working in and leading a diverse workforce requires excellent communication. Communication skills are any executive's, any manager's, any leader's most important skills. Understanding the meaning of communication is the first step to gaining those skills.

Defining Communication

Communication means understanding each other as individuals and as members of larger groups. It is the foundation of community.

Community has two primary meanings: geographic and social. A geographic community is an area defined by physical borders where people live and work. It is a neighborhood, a town, a state, or a country. All geographic communities consist of physical areas within which people have certain shared interests, including maintaining the environment and protecting the community from outside forces. The community members must work together, come to agreement on many issues, all for the best of everyone.

They share the concerns and goals, and sometimes the values, of their communities.

A social community has "boundaries" of shared values or interests. The gay community, the African American community, the nonprofit community, the Buddhist community, the sports community are all social communities. Unlike the members of geographic communities, members of social communities can be located around the corner or around the world. Their membership is defined by shared concerns, goals, and values.

The Nature of Communication

Communication is the process of creating shared meaning. It is the process by which we become one with others with respect to specific meanings and specific understandings. We share a part of ourselves, our message, our meaning of words and behaviors, with another.

We all have different frameworks. We all come from different backgrounds, different experiences. What means one thing to one person means something different to another, so we need to work together to create a meaning we can share. By going through the process of creating a shared meaning, we come to understand each other, we communicate.

Communicating Yourself

Sharing a part of yourself also focuses on another important element of communication: what we communicate. No matter what else we may want to communicate, or what meaning we want to create and share, we always communicate ourselves. The basic principles of communication include two truisms: as human beings, everything we do communicates something to those who hear or see us; and the primary thing we communicate is ourselves. In other words, we cannot *not* communicate ourselves.

Language and Communication

The method we use to communicate is through language. Kenneth Burke defined language as symbolic action.[6] In other words, humans use language as a way to act, a way to live. Words are our reality. They shape everything we understand and create things we don't see. Later in this book, we will look at how using words creates the reality that *girls* cannot become fire*men,* among other things. When we look at creating our visions and organizational culture (Chapter Eight), the importance of language as reality will become more apparent. A leader who can use language to create reality by communicating a vision of reality is a powerful leader indeed.

Diversity Tips

1. Diversity is a fact of contemporary organizational life and will become increasingly so in the future.

2. When positively and properly supported, workplace diversity can produce tangible benefits.

3. While leadership can come from any level in an organization, positive results are most likely to result when leadership comes from the top.

4. Communication and awareness are key.

2

Issues in Diversity

*Racial diversity in the workplace may get plenty
of lip service, but in private, minorities say they
can't break through the old-boy barriers, while
whites simmer over what they see as reverse
discrimination.*

San Francisco Chronicle[1]

Jason worked in a city office. For twelve of
his sixteen years there, the office had a
director who hired and promoted people based
on what he thought was merit. Four years ago
the director retired and the city manager hired
a woman from another government agency to
replace him. The new director threw out the
old hiring and promotion policies and brought
in a new approach.

When the new director came in, only a few women worked in supervisory positions in the office. There was one African American supervisor and no Latinos or Asians. Throughout the office there was only one Asian, three African Americans, and two Latinos. Under the new director only one of twenty-five positions filled in the past four years went to a white man. All other hires were African American, Asian, and Latino men, and women from several cultures. Of twelve promotions, none went to white men.

Jason and many of his friends reacted to the changes. They openly showed their disdain for new employees. They refused to help them, as they had helped new employees in the past. They failed to obey their new supervisors' instructions, reasoning that most of them had less experience than they did. The cultural and gender differences caused communication problems that led to misunderstandings. Racial rifts and sexual tensions heightened. When the newspapers got wind of problems in the office, the Director was forced to hire outside consultants to help resolve the inflamed situation.

UNDERSTANDING DIVERSITY ISSUES

The workplace is society in a microcosm, and it tends to reflect the issues, concerns, and tensions in society at large. It also brings many such issues to a particular focus. An executive needs to understand what these issues are to be able to respond to potential positive forces, recognize problems, and, in general, lead effectively.

Race

A person's race and ethnic characteristics, such as skin color and accent, can be the center of a number of serious issues both in American society and in the workplace. Respect, equality, fair treatment, and understanding are major concerns. A young Native American accountant, for example, might feel that he or she isn't mentored and doesn't get other help like young white accountants because of his race.

Differing perspectives of race is another concern. African Americans, for instance, often say that whites don't understand the extent of the harm caused by racial discrimination, while whites tend to feel that race-related problems have, on the whole, been "solved" or that past grievances have largely been addressed satisfactorily. These differing perspectives reveal a serious lack of understanding between blacks and whites.

Ceridian Corporation, a Minneapolis-based electronics and information services firm, assures the retention of high-quality employees of color and women by offering career development assistance. The company's executives select high-potential people of color and women for succession planning. All managers must set diversity goals. The company also provides internships for inner-city students and recruits at black colleges.[2]

Culture

Culture refers to the system of beliefs, values, customs, and institutions that create a common identity and ways of behavior for a given people. Cultural issues include different styles of communication and behavior, misunderstandings concerning favoritism, uses of time, and family matters.

Many people confuse racial and cultural issues because they often involve the same groups. Does a Native American accountant not find a mentor because the established accountants don't like the color of his skin or because the other accountants in the office don't understand his culture? Perhaps he is from a tribal group that does not like to be complimented in public in front of peers. The young accountant's displeasure over a compliment might lead the person who complimented him to think he doesn't want to associate with her.

Gender

Issues involving gender in the workplace include different communication styles, perceptions of values, equality of opportunity, sexual harassment, and other kinds of discrimination. Some of the discrimination is subtle. Some is not. Women complain about men asking inappropriate questions concerning family, among other things.

Another common complaint from women regards the lack of appreciation and respect. If they say something in a meeting, no one responds. Yet a few minutes later a man who makes the same suggestion will be praised for the quality of his input.

Sexual Harassment

Sexual harassment is one of the most pressing and costly problems facing organizations today. It is any unwelcome sexual advance of any kind, or any conduct related to gender that creates a hostile, offensive, or intimidating environment that no reasonable individual should have to endure. It is repeated, not asked for, and not returned. A 1988 study of Fortune 500 companies reported that sexual harassment caused low productivity, absenteeism, low morale, and employee turnover, which can cost an average-sized company up to $6.7 million a year.[3] (A more recent study put the figure at $8.7 million a year, or about $367 per employee.)[4]

Age

Age is the focus of a variety of issues, including the relevance of age (or lack thereof) to job performance and communication problems related to age differences. Some people wonder, for example, if the young marketing manager, Val, has enough experience to do the job as well as an older employee might. Others wonder why 65-year-old Bob is hanging onto his sales manager position so past his "prime."

Sexual Orientation

In recent years gays and lesbians increasingly have gone public and made their presence known in organizations, and the result has sometimes been conflict. Some people believe that homosexuality is immoral. Others just don't understand it. Support for nontraditional families—with respect to insurance coverage, for example—has become an issue. As these issues have surfaced, the tensions between gays and heterosexuals have similarly increased, sometimes to the point of violence.

Physical Characteristics

The Americans with Disabilities Act of 1990 assures workplace protections for people with disabilities. Many of their issues deal with physical barriers, yet many involve communication. In a workplace where work is manual, for example, deaf people complain about inequality. Non-deaf workers can talk while they work, but the deaf workers who communicate through sign language can't because their hands are occupied. If they do stop to talk with their hands, they are accused of slacking off, while hearing people who chat while working might be totally distracted by the conversation but not be called to task. Deaf people also don't have access to office gossip. They might have interpreters for staff meetings, but that is about it. They feel left out of office culture.

Reverse Discrimination

One major societal and workplace diversity issue is a reaction to other diversity issues: reverse discrimination. Reverse discrimination is the belief that diversity policies have gone too far and that white men face discrimination today. However, males still outnumber women and people of color in nearly all positions of power and still, on the average, make more money than others in the same or similar positions. The Federal Glass Ceiling Commission reported in 1995, for instance, that 97 percent of Fortune 500 company senior managers are white, 95 percent of them male. The Commission also reported that African American male professionals make only 79 percent of what white men with similar degrees and positions make.[5]

Nevertheless, there is anecdotal evidence demonstrating that white men are held back from hirings and promotions in some organizations. This evidence fuels the issue of reverse discrimination. Many white men are also upset with the growing trend to stereotype white men as "angry white males." This stereotype troubles many men. No one likes to be dismissed as a stereotype.

Workplace Issues

Many diversity issues are specific to the workplace. Some of these include employee concerns about relationships with co-workers, management issues, affirmative action, and how much the organizational culture needs to change to accommodate diversity.

Employee Relations

Executives need to understand employee issues and concerns. The general issues workers most commonly mentioned in focus groups and questionnaires pertain to how people relate with each other in the workplace. They include:

- Respect—understanding respect and respecting each other
- Misunderstandings because of style differences
- Lack of understanding of religious beliefs and their effects on the workplace
- Not enough information on cultural backgrounds and differences
- Too many cliques
- Offensive jokes

- No safe haven to discuss diversity issues
- Too much emphasis placed on diversity
- Not enough emphasis placed on diversity

Isms in the Workplace

The following scenarios are composites of situations that have happened in various organizations. In one way or another they are reflections of "Isms"—discriminatory or narrow-minded attitudes manifest by inappropriate conduct. Some kinds of Isms are easily recognizable forms of bigotry and hatred, but others are more subtle, though potentially as destructive. Situations like these below are some of the kinds of situations in which Isms are seen by the employees.

Chueh-Kuang has worked in the same department for several years. Most of his coworkers think he is very friendly, and don't realize how offended he is at what they think are innocent jokes about his name, or that they frequently ask him what is the best Chinese restaurant in town.

Nancy's social life revolves around her church. Her beliefs are very important to her, and it is distressing to her to hear others using language she considers sacrilegious, or joking about their sexuality. When Christmas approaches, she decorates her work area with Christian symbols. She is afraid that the emphasis on multiculturalism means that she should no longer wish coworkers a "Merry Christmas," which doesn't seem fair or right to her.

Gene always got along with his coworkers at his previous position with another company, and expected the same when he got a job managing a department of a large charity. He is very open about the fact he is gay, and talked with his new coworkers about his partner. His new coworkers, however, didn't respond as he thought they would. They isolated him, making sure they didn't have to work on any projects with him. They snicker about his being gay in front of him, and make him the object of many jokes.

Carla, a biochemist, is the only woman on her team. Several of the men on the team find her hard to relate to.

They think her style is not "warm" or "feminine," and that she doesn't have a sense of humor. At times she is referred to as a "bitch," and one man has dubbed her "The Iceberg." He calls her that nickname to her face.

An older male manager refers to all the females who work with him as "dear," "honey," and "sweetheart." At one point, he verbally reprimanded one woman for her inadequate job performance. During the reprimand, he shook his finger at her and called her "Little Miss." The women object to his choice of words, but their complaints seem to go right past him. He just shrugs their comments off with "I'm just from another generation."

Organizational Concerns

Employees know that their issues need strong leadership from management. Executives must respond to that need, as well as to other management issues that diversity creates. As Richard Rosenberg, chairman of Bank of America, says, "Diversity has to be managed. It just doesn't manage itself."[6] When there is weak leadership and management of diversity within an organization, a variety of problems can arise. Among them are:

- Disruptions and low morale: Intergroup conflicts cause fights, distrust, hatred. Morale cannot stay high under such conditions. Production suffers.

- Limited creativity and innovation: Diversity can enhance creativity and innovation, but too often managers fail to make good use of the broad range of skills and perspectives among their workers.

- Miscommunication, misunderstandings, fear, prejudice and discrimination, disunity, and inefficiency: Executives need to create an environment in which employees feel good about coming to work. Bad communication, fear, and discrimination affect the whole organization and can destroy it.

- High employee turnover: Employees leave nonsupportive organizations in order to find a work environment that is supportive. Organizations waste millions of dollars every year hiring and training new employees.

- Inability to compete in recruiting the best new employees: Any organization that gets a reputation for high turnover and low morale because of diversity problems will have difficulty attracting the top employment candidates.

- Weakened customer base: As a company's reputation for diversity-related problems grows, or as an organization fails to recruit people from diverse backgrounds, the organization will limit its customer base.

Diversity and Affirmative Action

One of the biggest organizational issues concerning diversity is the confusion between Affirmative Action and diversity. Many people assume they are the same thing. They are not. Diversity means that one's workforce is made up of people from different backgrounds. It has nothing to do with federal policy.

The confusion comes from several places. People often assume that Affirmative Action creates diversity in organizations, rather than understanding that diversity reflects society. Some companies now use the term *Affirmative Action* and *diversity* interchangeably, which creates confusion among members of those organizations.

Confusion also occurs when employees from diverse backgrounds attend diversity training programs to improve how they work together. While diversity training supports Affirmative Action and helps assure its success, it differs from the federal Affirmative Action policy in several major ways. The chart on page 18 reveals those differences.

Diversity Training	Affirmative Action
Uses a variety of tools to help employees from different backgrounds work together	Sets goals in recruitment and hiring, and monitors compliance
A business decision made for economic reasons	Moral and legal decisions made for social reasons
Designed to increase productivity and profitability in businesses and organizations	Designed to combat prejudicial hiring practices
Helps prevent current and future discrimination	Corrects past discrimination

Drawing the Line

One final organizational issue concerns the degree to which organizations should accommodate different cultures. Workers and managers alike worry that overemphasizing diversity and forgetting about traditional values will hurt the organization. They ask: Do we accept all behaviors? How do we blend extremely contradictory values? When is enough enough? Where do we draw the line?

Not all behaviors and values are acceptable. Each organization develops its own values, and must be true to them. We must draw a line that protects the core values and integrity of the organization. These values should include flexibility in accommodating cultural differences, but there is a point where accommodation negatively affects the whole organization. The workplace is no place for child labor, for instance, no matter what the worker's cultural norm. Organizations cannot accept radically varying senses of time, inequitable treatment of women, or potentially harmful attitudes about safety.

Venues for Discussion

Many people worry about diversity issues in general. Some feel organizations place too much emphasis on accepting differences. Others feel there is not enough emphasis. There needs to be a venue to talk about these and other issues. Even if we feel an attitude or value is not acceptable, it is important to try to understand why that attitude exists, and to help the individual and the organization reach a reasonable accommodation.

By understanding issues of diversity, executives can help change problems to benefits. If we merely declare that something is unacceptable without trying to understand it, many more problems will develop.

Diversity Tips

1. Awareness is the first step in dealing with diversity issues.

2. Employees' feelings about diversity are deep and intense.

3. Demonstrating knowledge of issues helps to educate everyone.

4. Encouraging communication on diversity issues aids in their successful resolution.

5. Leadership in and management of diversity is the key.

3

Looking Inward: Tools for Self-Awareness

You must be the change you wish to see in the world.

Mahatma Ghandi

During a Gender Communication Training Workshop at a major petrochemical company, John, a senior manager, looked into himself and discovered how his socialization affected his performance in the workplace. At one time the company's culture was very male-dominated, but the organization had been hiring more women in increasingly vital jobs. John felt he had done a good job of accepting women, being the first engineering manager to have two women on one team.

During training sessions, John had a chance to take a good, hard look at his working relationships with women employees. He felt that these relations were cordial and mutually respectful. But he had to admit to himself that women had never been promoted out of his group to a management position. His reasons for not supporting women candidates for promotion had varied over the years from inability to travel (due to family responsibilities) to not being "tough enough" to relate well to male managers.

John had been raised to view women as different from men—not inferior, but with different talents. He put women on pedestals. Though all three of his daughters had gone to college, and one had been a high school track champion, he'd never encouraged his wife to work outside the home. He felt a woman's place was in the home. Searching deeper into his socialization, John realized that his expectations of women were quite different from his expectations of men at work, too. The people he recommended for promotions were always men. In his mind, they were the bread winners and needed to get the higher paying positions.

SELF-AWARENESS: THE FIRST STEP TO LEADING A DIVERSE ORGANIZATION

Leaders capitalize on their strengths and find ways to improve on their weaknesses. First and foremost you communicate yourself. To communicate yourself with confidence, as an executive and as a leader, you need to know yourself very well. You need self-awareness.

To be self-aware, you need to understand how you were socialized and what influences made you the person you are today. You need to know your cultural identity and your values, and you need to understand your perceptions—how they are formed, how they influence who you are, and how and what you communicate. And you need to be able to tolerate ambiguity to be sure that the differences created by diversity do not affect your judgment as you communicate.

Awareness of Socialization

How were you socialized? What influenced you as you were growing up and what continues to influence you today? Typical influences include family, personal experiences, education, friends, the media, and critical incidents or events. You can use the "Socialization and Ism Prism" to better understand your socialization.

The Socialization and Ism Prism

We all have biases, or "isms" in our belief systems. The Socialization and Ism Prism in Exhibit 3.1 helps us find out what they are and why we have them. The SIP helps us isolate a bias, spread it out, and look at the "colors" that make it up. The SIP uses questions about how we have been socialized to show us the origins of our beliefs, attitudes, and values.

EXHIBIT 3.1
SOCIALIZATION AND THE ISM PRISM

- Family influences
- Personal experiences
- Educational experiences
- Peer influences
- Media influences
- Critical incidents

Model Questions for Using the SIP. In the example below, the question "How do I feel about Native Americans?" is put into the prism. The prism allows you to fully explore your biases and their sources, and to understand them.

Using the following questions (or similar ones) look at your life's influences (this is the prism). What comes out the other side is how these influences have affected you.

(Continued)

EXHIBIT 3.1
SOCIALIZATION AND THE ISM PRISM *(Continued)*

How do I feel about Native Americans?

Family influences

- What were my parents' attitudes toward Native Americans?
- How about my other relatives?

Personal experiences

- Did I know any Native Americans?
- Did I see reservations as I traveled?
- Did I have other personal experiences with Native Americans?

Educational experiences

- What did I learn in history at school about Native Americans?

Peer influences

- Did I play Cowboys and Indians games as a child? How did playing or not playing affect me?
- What were my friends' attitudes about Native Americans?

Media influences

- What did TV tell me about Native Americans? Movies?
- What did I read in newspapers? Books? Other media?

Critical incidents

- What critical incidents happened during my life that might have affected or changed my view?

Prism results

- And now, how do I view Native Americans?

The Socialization and Ism Prism can be used to analyze your socialization about any diversity issue. The questions you ask yourself are not as important as the fact that you ask as many as you can in each subject area.

Examining Gender Socialization Using the SIP. The following Prism is devoted to gender socialization. It adds a few questions about workplace socialization.

Question: *What influenced me as a child and adolescent in relation to my gender?*

(Continued)

EXHIBIT 3.1
SOCIALIZATION AND THE ISM PRISM *(Concluded)*

Family influences

- What did my parents and other family members tell me that I should or should not do as a female or male?

Personal experiences

- What kinds of behaviors did the males and females around me exhibit?
- Was I ever praised for behaving as males or females are "supposed to behave" ?

Educational experiences

- What did teachers tell me?
- Were teachers ever surprised that I performed something well for someone of my gender?

Peer experiences

- What did peers tell me?
- Was I ever teased for behaviors others thought inappropriate for my gender?

Media influences

- What images of sex roles did the books, movies, TV shows, newspapers, magazines, music and other media portray?
- What toys, such as doctors' or nurses' kits, costumes for Halloween, etc., influenced me in terms of future career choices?

Critical incidents

- What critical incidents happened during my life that might have affected or changed my view?

Employment and Career

- How have my early thoughts about work influenced me in relation to my choice of careers, job performance, and my employment experiences?
- How did my parents' or guardians' jobs (or lack of jobs) influence me?
- What job role models and mentors did I have, and how did they influence my style at work?
- How did my first supervisor's attitudes about gender influence my style at work?
- How did my first coworkers' attitudes influence me?
- How do my current job experiences continue to influence my attitude about what a male or female employee should be like?

AWARENESS OF CULTURAL IDENTITY

Questions to Reveal Personal Assumptions

The following tool, an extension of the Ism Prism, turns the focus on your attitudes toward yourself.[1] Answer the questions to understand better who you are.

1. What are my co-cultures? (Include your race/ ethnicity, culture, nation of origin, gender, sexual orientation, age, physical abilities, class, and religion.) With which ones do I most strongly or closely identify? Which seem the least important to my identity? Why?

2. During what critical incident or time period did I initially became aware of my cultural identity?

3. Being my (race/ethnicity/culture/nationality) means:

4. Being male/female means:

5. Being my age means:

6. Being my religion means:

7. Having my physical abilities means:

8. Being my sexual orientation means:

9. Growing up poor/working class/middle-class/upper-class meant:

10. Some of the things I see as benefits from my background are:

11. Some liabilities (things I need to watch out for personally and in relationship to others) are:

12. What are some of the names used in referring to the cultural groups of which I am a member? Which ones are acceptable and unacceptable for me? How does hearing the unacceptable ones make me feel?

By answering the above questions, you have thought about who you are. Any tool that helps us examine ourselves improves our self-awareness.

AWARENESS OF VALUES

Another important aspect of self-awareness is our values. They define who we are as human beings. Our values determine our attitudes and behaviors. They concern what we consider good or bad, right or wrong, just or unjust.

Terminal and Instrumental Values

Milton Rokeach divides values into two types, terminal and instrumental. *Terminal values* are the end-states of existence that we desire, such as equality, freedom, and self-respect. *Instrumental values* are the ways we want to behave, such as being courageous, honest, and responsible. Once we understand what our values are, which ones are most important and shape how we approach the world, we will better understand how we behave and communicate in the world.

Exhibit 3.2 contains a tool to help you determine your hierarchy of values.[2] Follow the directions to explore your values.

Determining Your Hierarchy of Values

The survey in Exhibit 3.2 helps you understand which values are most important to you. Several human motivation theories suggest we tend to act in accordance with a hierarchy of values, with the most important values determining our behaviors. Others, such as cognitive dissonance theory, suggest that if we note a behavior that is in contradiction, or dissonance, with higher values, we will adapt to accommodate the dissonant event. Either way, it is vital to understand your hierarchy of values in order to be truly self-aware.

AWARENESS OF PERCEPTIONS

No matter what we intend to communicate, we communicate ourselves. Our socialization, cultural identity, and values are all a part of what we communicate to others. Another hidden, or not immediately apparent, aspect of ourselves is our perceptions.

EXHIBIT 3.2A
VALUES TEST

Rokeach Terminal Values

Directions: Place an "X" in the boxes reflecting the importance of the values listed on the left. Mark no more than six values as "Very Important."

Values	Not Important	Very Important	Neutral
A comfortable life (prosperity)	☐	☐	☐
An exciting life (stimulation, activity)	☐	☐	☐
A sense of accomplishment (lasting contribution)	☐	☐	☐
A world at peace (free of war)	☐	☐	☐
A world of beauty (natural and artistic beauty)	☐	☐	☐
Equality (fairness, equal opportunity for all)	☐	☐	☐
Family security (taking care of loved ones)	☐	☐	☐
Freedom (independence, free choice)	☐	☐	☐
Happiness (being contented)	☐	☐	☐
Inner harmony (freedom from inner conflict)	☐	☐	☐
Mature love (sexual and spiritual intimacy)	☐	☐	☐
National security (protection from attack)	☐	☐	☐
Pleasure (an enjoyable, leisurely life)	☐	☐	☐
Salvation (eternal life, worship)	☐	☐	☐
Self-respect (self-esteem)	☐	☐	☐
Social recognition (respect, admiration)	☐	☐	☐
True friendship (close companionship)	☐	☐	☐
Wisdom (mature understanding of life)	☐	☐	☐

EXHIBIT 3.2B
VALUES TEST

Rokeach Instrumental Values

DIRECTIONS: Place an "X" in the boxes reflecting the importance of the values listed on the left. Mark no more than six values as "Very Important."

Values	Not Important	Very Important	Neutral
Ambitious (hardworking)	☐	☐	☐
Broad (or open)-minded	☐	☐	☐
Capable (competent, effective)	☐	☐	☐
Cheerful (joyful)	☐	☐	☐
Clean (neat)	☐	☐	☐
Courageous (standing up for beliefs)	☐	☐	☐
Forgiving (willing to pardon others)	☐	☐	☐
Helpful (working for others' welfare)	☐	☐	☐
Honest (genuine, truthful)	☐	☐	☐
Imaginative (creative, innovative)	☐	☐	☐
Independent (self-sufficient)	☐	☐	☐
Intellectual (intelligent, reflective)	☐	☐	☐
Logical (consistent, rational)	☐	☐	☐
Loving (affectionate)	☐	☐	☐
Obedient (dutiful, respectful)	☐	☐	☐
Polite (courteous)	☐	☐	☐
Responsible (dependable)	☐	☐	☐
Self-controlled (self-disciplined)	☐	☐	☐

Source: Milton Rokeach, *Beliefs, Attitudes and Values* (San Francisco: Jossey-Bass, Inc., Publishers, 1968), and *The Nature of Human Values* (New York: Free Press, 1973).

Defining Perceptions

Perception is the process of selecting, organizing, and interpreting the world. It is how we become aware of what is around us. We all have different experiences and different backgrounds that lead to our different perceptions, different ways of seeing the world, and different ways of thinking. Our experience and culture determine what input we accept as reality, and what input we simply ignore because it doesn't fit within our world view. Because of differences in perception, we often *do not* see what *does* exist and *do* see what *does not* exist.

Selecting What We See

Since it is impossible for us to consciously pay attention to all the sensory information we receive, we naturally screen much of it out. Four factors are involved in selecting what we see: selective attention, selective exposure, selective recall, and first impressions.

Selective Attention. We tend to notice some things and not others. There is too much information coming into our brains to notice or pay attention to all of it. When we are in a situation that is new to us, many things compete for our attention. Both consciously and unconsciously, we tend to choose what to pay attention to based on our own background.

Selective Exposure. People tend to notice favorable and familiar things and to avoid unpleasant and unfamiliar ones. For instance, many people do not like conflict and choose not to notice when the workplace is filled with conflict or unpleasantness. They might, for example, notice one black male who appears to get along well in a managerial position and not notice how few black males are in managerial positions.

Selective Recall. We tend to remember some things and forget others. In particular, we tend to forget episodes that are inconsistent with our present self-image or to revise our memory to better reflect our current self-image. We might have a horrible day at the office, where almost everything goes wrong, except for one major deal we signed. We will remember the day as being a good one, even though the bad things that happened might come back to haunt us.

First Impressions. Our first impressions tend to strongly influence our later impressions. Nevertheless, as an executive, it is imperative to be flexible enough to change your perceptions and to understand that first impressions do not tell the whole story. This is especially true when dealing with diversity. You might see or hear something and make a negative assumption about its meaning. It may be, though, that the communicator's background is so different from yours that what she meant was not what you thought (from your own experience) she meant. It's necessary to realize that a first impression is just that—a single impression that gives no more than a part of the total picture.

Organizing Sensory Data

Once we have narrowed the amount of sensory data to pay attention to, we organize and classify it. Four characteristics of this organizational process that are of particular importance: stereotyping, polarization, self-fulfilling prophecy, and consistency.

Stereotyping. Stereotyping concerns the psychological need humans have to organize and categorize their perceptions. We have a need to generalize or to assume the existence of certain traits so that we can communicate. We cannot reinvent the wheel every time we meet someone. We need to be able to assume certain things about people based on our past experiences with people "like them." Perhaps it is their smile, how they say things, what their cultural background is. But we also need to be flexible. When these generalizations become fixed, rigid, or oversimplified, we often create fixed, rigid pictures of people that make it difficult to look at them as individuals.

Exhibit 3.3 is an exercise designed to look at gender stereotypes. By doing the exercise, you will become aware of the types of stereotypes you may hold concerning gender.

EXHIBIT 3.3
EXPLORING GENDER STEREOTYPES

Job titles often refer to or imply the gender of the worker. After each of the following titles, place an "M" (for man) or "W" (for woman), depending on what gender the title indicates to you.

1. Secretary _____

2. Electrician _____

3. Engineer _____

4. Nurse _____

5. Technician _____

Many people view the same behavior in women and men as being different, and use stereotypical descriptions to express those attitudes. For instance, a man is called a "bachelor," while a woman is a "spinster," and where a man suffers a "mid-life crisis," a woman is "menopausal."

In the following examples, determine the stereotype and fill in each blank with a W (for women) or an M (for men).

_____ are nosy   _____ are curious

_____ are firm   _____ are stubborn

_____ are ambitious   _____ are pushy

_____ are scattered   _____ are versatile

_____ are concerned   _____ are anxious

_____ are domineering   _____ are strong

Many people attribute certain personality characteristics to men and women.

Which of the following are more stereotypically associated with either gender? Fill in each blank with a W (for woman) or an M (for man).

1. Talkative _____

2. Deliberate _____

3. Emotional _____

4. Sensitive _____

5. Aggressive _____

Polarization. Polarization means perceiving things in terms of extremes and categorizing people into opposites. We have a legitimate need to "organize" the world. The trick is finding enough of the right categories. Most things, most people are somewhere in between the extremes. In a diverse organization it is easy to fall into this trap. For instance, we might think that a man who doesn't date women must be gay, or that the new Director of Information Systems must be non-Christian because she takes a holiday for Kwaanza.

Self-Fulfilling Prophecy. Self-fulfilling prophecy is the tendency to align our perceptions to match our expectations. Things turn out the way we say they will because we do everything possible, often subconsciously, to make them turn out that way. We see a person in a wheelchair and assume he can't get the job done without help. So we offer help, constantly, to the point that the person expects the help or cannot do the job without the help because he has not had the opportunity to learn through experience how to do the job.

Consistency Theory. Consistency theory is a system of telling us what belief systems and personality traits go together in a person. Our perceptions relate to our logic. We make assumptions or deductions about people based on their belief systems and personality traits. We might note that a man smiles a lot, is nice to us, works well with others, and from these traits assume he will be as effective with—or nice to—a person whose background differs from ours.

Interpreting Sensory Data

After we select and organize sensory data, we interpret it and attach meaning to it. Two aspects of interpreting sensory data are fact-inference confusion and frame of reference.

Fact-Inference Confusion. When we see something, we tend to immediately make inferences—assumptions or judgments—about the facts. Our perceptions are influenced by these inferences. If we are working with a person who doesn't speak English very well, we might infer that she needs help understanding written instructions. This may or may not be true. Inferences are natural and important, but we must understand that they are inferences, not facts. In such cases we need more information before making our final conclusion.

Frame of Reference. Our frame of reference is the individual set of attitudes, experiences, education, and skills that make us tend to interpret sensory data in habitual or predetermined ways. Within families, age groups, cultural groups, etc., frames of reference are similar though never identical; each person's frame of reference is unique. We impose our frame of reference on our perceptions. It becomes the screen through which see and interpret the world.

A person's Jewish heritage, for example, influences his or her perception of the need to accept non-Christian holidays. A man's experience as a father and husband influences his perceptions of information concerning paternity leave. Our frame of reference demonstrates the need to understand our socialization and cultural identity in order to understand our perceptions.

Understanding Your Perceptions

One way to understand your perceptions is to try out a few observations. Ask yourself: "What is the first thing that comes to mind when I hear the word *diversity*? What is my judgment or evaluation of the image I see? Is it positive or negative? Where did the image come from?" Do this for a few other items. Just think of something, and immediately think of an image. Doing this exercise, you will become more aware of your perceptions and where they came from, and help yourself become more self-aware.

Learning How Others Perceive Us

By gaining an understanding of how different people from different facets of our lives and from different backgrounds see us, we gain a fuller, more balanced view of our total selves. We need to ask others questions about ourselves, and we need to listen to the answers we receive. The perceptions of others, even if incorrect, say something about who we are. Looking at *why* people perceive us in certain ways adds to our self-understanding. We learn more about our strengths as well as more about areas in which we need improvement.

Another way to learn about how others perceive you is to self-disclose. Tell someone something about yourself they may not know. Chances are, you will receive feedback about what you disclosed, and possibly other information about that person's perceptions of you, as well. Self-disclosure will be discussed more later in the book.

SELF-AWARENESS TOOL: ROLLING THE D.I.E.

It is one thing to know that we occasionally stereotype or that we select the reality we want to see, and another thing to do something about it. Understanding how perceptions work does not mean that we are always aware of our own perceptions. For checking perceptions, there is a useful tool commonly called Rolling the D.I.E.: Describe, Interpret, Evaluate. (See Exhibit 3.4)

The D.I.E. forces us to look into ourselves to determine why we hold certain beliefs or why we interpret things in a particular way. It also is an excellent tool for learning about others and for communicating to others. As you "roll" the D.I.E., think about how the tool might help you, as an executive, understand and communicate to others. As you read the following two chapters, you may want to refer back to the D.I.E.

Exhibit 3.4 explains the terms that D.I.E. stands for, followed by a sample "rolling" of the D.I.E. to show you how it works.

Rolling the D.I.E. as a Self-Awareness Tool

The Rolling the D.I.E. tool can be used as an everyday tool to help you remove yourself emotionally from a scene at work. It gives you a chance to "count to ten." Describe what you are experiencing to yourself as well as you can. Then interpret what

---

EXHIBIT 3.4
ROLLING THE D.I.E.

Description: The information we gather when we *see, hear, smell, touch,* and *taste.* Because our physical senses vary to some degree, none of us see, hear, smell, touch, or taste exactly the same ways.

Interpretation: What we *think* about what we see, hear, smell, touch, and taste. Because of our different backgrounds, experiences, styles, and skills, our ways of thinking and processing information differ.

Evaluation: What we *feel* about what we think, and what kind of assessment of value—positive, negative, or neutral—we attach to our interpretations. Because we have diverse value systems, we all make different evaluations of our observations.

Rolling the D.I.E.

Imagine that you are in the midst of a conversation with a coworker and his or her eyes never meet yours. Depending upon your own value system you might:

- Describe this experience by saying:
  Sarah did not make eye contact with me.

- Interpret this experience as meaning:
  Sarah wasn't very interested in what I was telling her.

- Evaluate this experience by feeling:
  Sarah is rude.

Alternately you might:

- Describe this experience by saying:
  Sarah did not make eye contact with me.

- Interpret this experience as meaning:
  Sarah was embarrassed.

- Evaluate this experience by feeling:
  Sarah is shy.

---

you have described. Interpret it several ways, as many ways as possible. Note the differences. By looking at alternate interpretations, you will not jump to conclusions. You might never get to the evaluative state. For practice, try the exercise in Exhibit 3.5.

EXHIBIT 3.5
ROLLING THE D.I.E. EXERCISE

Observe three scenes at your workplace and write down what you notice. Distinguish between describing, interpreting, and evaluating what you observe in the scenes. For each of the three scenes, answer the following questions:

- What did you observe?
- Which observations were Descriptions? Interpretations? Evaluations?
- What are some alternative interpretations of each scene?

Tolerance for Ambiguity

Rolling the D.I.E. will also help increase your tolerance for ambiguity. When working with people from diverse backgrounds, what you think you see might not be the reality. People say things with meanings other than what you might assume. Words are ambiguous by their very nature; they have more than one meaning and can be used in many contexts. As discussed in the perceptions section above, our frames of reference also lead to different understandings of the same situation.

All of these things lead to ambiguity. To be a good communicator in a diverse workplace, you must have a tolerance for ambiguity. By using the D.I.E., you step back from your assumptions and understand that ambiguities might be present. It gives you time to analyze the situation, and helps you better understand the intended meaning.

SELF-AWARENESS IS SELF-IMPROVEMENT

Leaders stay ahead by working on improving themselves. One type of self-improvement to work on, especially as an executive in a diverse organization, is to commit yourself to the lifelong journey of understanding yourself and the diverse world around you.

No matter how hard we try, we all have biases. When you wake up tomorrow morning, try wondering what prejudice you will discover during the day, what assumption you will make that will be proven wrong, what bias will affect your day. By finding at least one bias a day, you will know you are continually working on self-awareness. You will show yourself that you are self-aware enough to know that you have biases, and are working at eliminating as many as possible. When you continually work on self-awareness, you become aware of things that are happening around you and are able to intervene and take on a leadership role.

The experiences of Ernest Drew, former CEO of Hoechst Celanese Chemical Company, are a good example. Drew had always viewed diversity in terms of numbers of employees, as Affirmative Action, that is, until he attended a conference of his company's top officers.

The conference included 125 top company officers, who were primarily white males, plus an additional 50 women and people of color from lower-level positions in the company. Attendees split into problem-solving teams, some diverse, some all white male. All teams discussed the same question: How does the corporate culture affect business, and what changes might be made to improve results.

The teams' findings changed the way Drew looked at diversity. The diverse teams had broader solutions, including ideas that Drew had never thought of. He became aware of what diversity could mean to his company and how his own restricted views had held back the company's progress. After that conference Drew knew he needed diversity at every level of his organization. As proof of his commitment to diversity, he created a diverse group to staff the company's polyester textile filament division, which had lost money for 18 straight years. With a series of dramatic moves, the division was earning a profit within 5 years.[3]

Diversity Self-Awareness Questionnaire

The questionnaire in Exhibit 3.6 can help you work on your self-awareness by examining your communication skills in relation to diversity. You will better understand what areas you need to work on in order to become a better communicator and a more effective executive in your diverse organization.

EXHIBIT 3.6
DIVERSITY QUESTIONNAIRE

Instructions: Place a number next to each question that best describes your own actions and beliefs.

1 = almost always   2 = frequently   3 = sometimes
4 = seldom   5 = almost never

1. _____ Do you recognize and challenge the perceptions, assumptions, and biases that affect your thinking?

2. _____ Do you think about the impact of what you say or how you act before you speak or act?

3. _____ Do you do everything you can to prevent the reinforcement of prejudices, including avoiding using negative stereotypes when you speak?

4. _____ Do you demonstrate your respect for people who are not from the dominant culture by doing things that show you feel they are as competent and skilled as others, including handing them responsibility as often as you do others?

5. _____ Do you encourage people who are not from the dominant culture to speak out on their concerns and respect those issues?

6. _____ Do you speak up when someone is making racial, sexual, or other derogatory remarks, or is humiliating another person?

7. _____ Do you apologize when you realize you might have offended someone due to inappropriate behavior or comments?

8. _____ Do you try to know people as individuals, not as representatives of specific groups, and include different types of people in your peer group?

9. _____ Do you accept the notion that people from all backgrounds have a need to socialize with and reinforce one another?

(Continued)

EXHIBIT 3.6
DIVERSITY QUESTIONNAIRE *(Concluded)*

10. _____ Do you do everything that you can to understand your own background, and try to educate yourself about other backgrounds, including different communication styles?

SCORING: The lower your score, the better you communicate and improve the climate in your diverse organization and the community at large. To improve your communication, increase your use of the behaviors listed.

Diversity Tips

1. An understanding of what influenced your socialization helps you to be aware of the attitudes you bring to the workplace.

2. Knowing your cultural identity and understanding what that identity brings to your communication helps you communicate with others of differing cultural identities.

3. Determining your hierarchy of values helps in understanding how you behave and communicate.

4. Awareness of your perceptions and their influence on your communication helps you to communicate more effectively.

5. Asking others questions about yourself and listening to the answers aids in self-awareness.

6. Waiting before you react to differentiate between observations, interpretations, and evaluations helps you to avoid jumping to conclusions and respond appropriately.

7. Constantly working on your self-awareness and your understanding of diversity is a mark of effective leadership.

4

Looking Outward: Understanding People from Diverse Backgrounds

Managers are responsible for creating a work environment in which the contributions of all people are recognized. To do this, they need to understand how to best utilize individual differences so that people's special attributes can be used to achieve company objectives.

John Young
Former President and CEO
of Hewlett-Packard

A large philanthropic foundation recently hired Henry, an African American, as a manager. He had worked successfully as a manager in a similar organization in an African American community. Now he is the only black man at his new organization.

Henry faces several difficulties at the foundation. He knows he is responsible for the quality of work and the output of his division, yet he feels great resistance to his attempts to motivate the people who work under him. They say they don't understand Henry or his suggestions. Recently, one of Henry's most talented employees challenged his leadership in a large meeting.

Henry is thinking of quitting. He performs his job well but is tired of people acting unfriendly and hostile. He doesn't want to fail, though. The challenges of the job excite him, and he wants to make the most of living in his new community. He has asked his supervisor for a meeting to discuss the situation. He wants to go in and show her just how good a manager he is and tell her that people need time to adjust to his style. Mostly, Henry wants respect for who he is.

Communication styles differ between cultures. Many of the problems Henry is having communicating to people in his new organization probably relate to his being the only black man in the organization. Understanding and respecting each others' different styles and being tolerant of different styles is crucial to being a good communicator and an effective executive in a diverse organization. To understand differences, we need to respect and appreciate our differences in communication style, background, and values, tolerate what is not easy to understand, and be flexible in adapting to new communication situations.

LISTENING FOR UNDERSTANDING

Listening is the best way to determine which issues are important, what problems exist, and how your leadership skills can help people. People often misunderstand listening. Listening is a skill that needs development, honing, and constant attention. To listen well requires effort. In fact, some people who cannot physically hear well are better listeners than people with perfect hearing, because they work at listening.

Listening Styles

Each of us listens differently and develops our own individual style of listening. Each culture listens differently from others. In the United States, one of the telling differences in listening styles is between women and men.

The "masculine" style of listening tends to be analytical and problem-solving. When most men listen, they interrupt and offer advice to the speaker. They also listen to jockey for position, to compete. Most women, on the other hand, listen empathically (though Sam Keen notes in *Fire in the Belly* that men are becoming more and more empathic in their listening styles[1]). The "feminine" style of listening shows support for the speaker. Some men think women listeners agree with them because they nod their heads, when in reality they are only being supportive. Women tend to use listening as a means to network.

Obstacles to Effective Listening

To become good listeners, we first must work on understanding the obstacles to good listening. The list below includes the major obstacles to effective listening, and some of the specific difficulties in listening to people from different backgrounds.

1. Allowing your attitude about the speaker to influence what you hear: This is especially true when communicating with someone whose background affects you. For instance, when listening to someone older or younger than you, you might have an attitude about a person "that age" which causes a reaction that prevents you from really listening.

2. Allowing your beliefs and attitudes toward the topic to interfere with your listening: People from diverse backgrounds may see the same workplace topic with quite different perspectives. When you talk with a colleague about a new technology, for example, your reaction to the topic might relate to your

culture, and that reaction might prevent you from really hearing what the other person is saying about the technology.

3. Getting emotionally upset over something that is said, or allowing your feelings to affect your listening in a negative way: Communicating with a person whose perspective is quite different from your own can be frustrating, even overwhelming. You might be so angered by what is said that you stop listening, or you might feel so sorry for the person that your sympathy gets in the way of listening to what is said.

4. Hearing what you expect to hear rather than listening to what is being said: We might have certain expectations when listening to someone from a particular background, and will hear what we expect to hear at the cost of not listening to what is actually being communicated. We might expect a person with a disability to be in favor of wheelchair ramps and maybe not hear her saying the space in the lab is too small to accommodate ramps.

5. Listening only for literal meanings rather than hidden or underlying meanings: What is said is not always what is meant. For instance, when communicating with a person who speaks English as a second language, the person might directly translate an idiom from her or his first language. The idiom might mean something entirely different in English. Or, the person's communication style might be to say things literally but to mean them figuratively.

6. Focusing only on the delivery and nonverbal communication of the speaker: Not only can this be distracting, preventing you from hearing everything that is said, but with issues of diversity, especially cultural issues, the smallest details of the message might be important. Perhaps more importantly, the delivery and nonverbal communication of the speaker might be so different from your life experience that the communication is misunderstood. Nonverbal communication will be more fully discussed later in this chapter.

7. Listening only for the facts: Listening only for the facts can be dangerous because often the feelings of the speaker are as important as the facts. Also, the person might come from a culture that defines facts differently from you, or might present facts in ways you might not be familiar with.

8. Being so concerned about your own performance (what you will say and how you will say it) that you miss part of what the speaker is saying: A common problem in listening is thinking of how you might respond to the person talking. When a speaker is culturally different, she or he might have a sense of inferiority, or feel ill at ease. When confidence is not as high as it should be, it can be difficult to listen to other people. It can also be difficult when there is too much competition, and the listener is thinking of ways to come back to the speaker, to "win" the communication event.

9. Letting the speaker do all the work, rather than listening actively: If the listener doesn't work at listening, she or he isn't fully engaged in the communication, and may miss an important piece of information. When differences exist, it is imperative to play as active a role as possible to share in the creation of meaning to communicate successfully.

ACTIVE LISTENING

Active Listening is a tool both for becoming a better listener and for gaining better understanding of others. Active Listening means listening to and trying to understand the speaker's thoughts *and* feelings by restating, or paraphrasing, as closely as possible, what the speaker has said. In other words, listening so that you can repeat, as a paraphrase, everything the person who has spoken has said, without interpretations, comments, and so on. Just what the person said, no more, no less.

Active Listening as a Managerial Tool

When we use Active Listening, we try to understand exactly what the person who is talking is saying to us. We give the speaker control over what is being communicated, but we remain active by making sure we understand the communication.

Active Listening can be used as a specific leadership or managerial tool. Paraphrasing for the speaker shows him or her that you are conscientious about understanding what they are saying. If she is below you in the organization, Active Listening can motivate her, show her you care about her input, and that she is a valuable member of your team. If the person is above you in the organization, Active Listening shows respect. Active Listening shows that you want to be sure you do the best job you can. In general, when a leader or manager uses Active Listening, she empowers the people she is listening to, and assures that communication takes place and the job gets done.

Active Listening Mode

There are several ways an executive can use Active Listening. One way is to go into "Active Listening mode." Listen, then paraphrase. You might tell the speaker that you are practicing Active Listening. You can make it seem more natural by telling the speaker: "I really want to be sure I understand your point, so I will repeat back to you what you say." Don't say anything while the speaker talks. Do not respond, ask questions, or interrupt. Try not to let what you hear affect you emotionally or in any other way. Do not interpret, analyze, or evaluate what is said. When the speaker finishes, paraphrase back to him what you heard, as closely as possible, and ask if you heard correctly. If you did, then let the speaker talk again. If he feels you are not understanding the communication, let him clarify.

Active Listening for Understanding and Respect

We can use Active Listening to find out specific things about others that lead to better understanding. When you listen to someone talk about her background, what holidays she might like, for instance, or what aspects of her culture she likes the most, you begin to understand more about who she is and where she came from. You begin to understand commonalities as well as differences.

When developing training programs for organizations, some companies often do Active Listening as a small group exercise. The exercise in Exhibit 4.1 can be used to help participants understand what being respected means to us, and how we like to be treated. The exercise also elicits participants' perceptions concerning how much respect exists in their workplace, and what kinds of organizational support are in place to honor those senses of respect. This exercise can be modified to do one-on-one.

EXHIBIT 4.1
LISTENING FOR RESPECT

We all want to be treated with respect at the workplace and elsewhere. Yet, being treated with respect means different things to different people. You will be asked to discuss, in a small group, what being respected at the workplace means to you. To help prepare you for that discussion, think about the following questions.

- What does being treated with respect mean to you?
- How do you feel or react when you are treated with respect?
- How do you feel or react when you aren't treated with respect?
- How do you want people to approach you if they have a problem with you (perhaps with a mistake you have made, or because you have offended them)?

Groups are then given the following instructions:

- In small groups, you will be discussing what being respected in the workplace means to you.
- We will divide into groups of six, and divide each of those groups into groups of three.
- One of the three-person groups will talk among themselves for six minutes, while the other group of three listens. Then the listening group will summarize (for five minutes and to the speaking groups' satisfaction) what was said, both verbally and nonverbally. They should also summarize what they sensed the speakers were feeling as they spoke.
- The listening group will now become the speaking group, the speaking group will become the listeners, and we will repeat the process.

The speakers should:

- Focus only on the people they are talking to.
- Get into it. Feel what they say and say it strongly.
- Talk about all aspects of being respected in the workplace.

(Continued)

EXHIBIT 4.1
LISTENING FOR RESPECT *(Concluded)*

The listeners should:

- Not ask questions or say anything.
- Make an effort to not let what they hear affect their emotions.
- Not analyze, evaluate, or interpret what they hear.
- Try to remember everything that is said.
- Try to sense what the speakers are feeling.
- Pay attention to nonverbal communication.

After the exercise, the participants are debriefed with the following questions.

- What similarities of experience and/or feelings did you find as you listened to the other people?
- What about differences?
- How does an individual who consistently isn't treated with respect at work feel? What are the consequences?
- What are the consequences for an individual who consistently doesn't treat others with respect?
- Do you feel that employees treating each other with respect is a part of the mainstream of your organizational culture?

Other Active Listening Exercises

You can tailor your own Active Listening exercise based upon your workplace's concerns. Here are some suggestions:

- Create a group of people from one ethnic group and pair them with a group of people with another ethnicity. The first group talks among itself about its culture, and what being of that culture in this society means. The other group listens, paraphrases, and learns about both their commonalities and differences. Then the groups switch roles.

    For instance, in 1993 one company's Systems Storage Division, located in San Jose, California, launched a Diversity Day. The city boasts a very diverse population (33 languages are spoken), and the Division's workforce reflects that diversity. It was decided to launch the special event in the hopes of helping its employees understand each others' cultures. Employees dressed in ethnic clothes, did traditional dances, and shared cultural foods. The event was so successful in defusing tensions between groups that Diversity Day is now an annual event, and the Division's Diversity Council prepares a monthly bulletin listing diversity events in the city.[2]

- Do the same exercise as a one-on-one. Pair two people of differing ethnicity and have each, in turn practice Active Listening as they discuss their individual cultures.

- Try the same exercises for people with disabilities, different age groups, or women and men.

- The exercise can also be used for a specific diversity issue, like the one on respect that opened this section. For sexual harassment, have people discuss their experiences and feelings about sexual harassment as a man or woman. Have them include times they realize they may have been a harasser, and times they perceived a person as having "encouraged" sexual harassment. If they feel they have never experienced sexual harassment, have them talk about what they have observed.

Darrel Ray, President of Consulting Services, in Shawnee Mission, Kansas, relates how other variations of Active Listening can resolve problems. A dysfunctional group, comprised of five black men and five white women, was supposed to process credit card insurance claims for a financial services company. But there was no communication or cooperation—and no productivity. The team facilitator held a meeting in which members aired their differences and grievances. Three hours of yelling, but also of expressing fears, stereotypes, and assumptions they had about one another enabled members to work together. A month later the group's productivity increased significantly, and group members were even socializing after work.[3]

EMPATHY AND READING NONVERBAL
COMMUNICATION

Listening is not only hearing. It also means trying to feel what the speaker is feeling, what we sometimes refer to as empathy. And it means being able to read the nonverbal communication of the speaker, everything that surrounds or replaces the words.

Empathy

Empathy is the skill of feeling what another feels. We can never completely walk inside another person's shoes, but we can work on this skill to the point where we can approach that feeling.

Many confuse empathy with sympathy, but they are quite different. When we sympathize, we feel for the other person, but we do not necessarily try to understand how or what she feels. Empathy doesn't rely on liking or believing in what the other person thinks or feels. Empathy does not depend on sympathy. It depends on understanding. A woman with disabilities doesn't want your sympathy, but you can feel empathy for her. You can empathize with her problems, understand her needs, and understand how best to communicate with her. A gay manager trying to communicate with a homophobic employee, for example, needs to understand the employee in order to communicate with him and motivate him to perform his job.

Empathy for Differences

There are specific methods to help us empathize with people different from us. One is to do something in a way that is very different from the way you usually do that thing, somehow make it public, and think about people who are always doing things that seem different to the dominant culture. One of the best exercises I have seen in this regard is Right Hand/Left Hand, shown in Exhibit 4.2. I've adapted Gardenschwartz and Rowe's version of this exercise from their *The Diversity Tool Kit*.[4]

EXHIBIT 4.2
RIGHT HAND/LEFT HAND

Using your nondominant hand, perform the following tasks:

- Write this sentence: The sun is shining on the treetops.
- Write today's date.
- Sign your name.
- Draw a tree.
- If you are doing this exercise with other people, show them your work.

Questions:

1. How did you feel doing these tasks with your nondominant hand?
2. How would you feel if you had to use your nondominant hand at work all the time?
3. What tasks would be easier for you to do with your nondominant hand? Harder?
4. How long would it take you to become as proficient with your nondominant hand as you are with your dominant one?
5. What would you do if your job consisted almost entirely of the more difficult tasks?
6. How do you think your boss would evaluate your performance? What if you were compared to others who could work with their dominant hand?
7. What hand would you use when no one was looking? When the boss wasn't around? At home?
8. What does this suggest about language differences (and other differences) on the job?
9. How would you assist people who are working in some way with their "nondominant hand"?

Role Playing for Empathy

Role playing is another tool to improve empathy. Taking on the role of someone else allows the freedom to act out in a given situation. By acting out what you think are the thoughts, feelings, and behavior of others, you better understand them, and gain a clearer understanding of your own behavior and feelings. We will look at two different types of role-playing: role-reversals and cultural role-playing.

Role-Reversals. One example of Role-Reversal is Gender Role-Reversal, where a man takes on a woman's role and a woman takes on a man's. A typical gender role-reversal might deal with sexual harassment.

When doing the Role Play, act out your roles. Do what you think the other sex would do in that situation. Feel it, and react to what the other person is doing. When you are done, discuss how each of you acted. How did each of you feel seeing how the other person perceived your sex would act?

Cultural Role Playing. For my Diversity Management Games course, I developed the following Cultural Role Play. In this course, the students and I first discuss what constitutes culture. Students then break into small groups to create unique English-speaking cultures. These cultures are based on shared values and communication idiosyncrasies. (For example, one group may form a culture based on love of nature in which the word *green* has a variety of spiritual meanings. When members of this group speak with other people, they always look down in order to draw strength from the earth.) Students then go through a series of two-person, small group and large group management role plays in which they represent their newly formed cultures.

With the above exercise, participants begin to understand what being from a different culture feels like. Rules are unknown, language is a barrier (even when they speak the same language), and there are many other forms of discomfort. By creating a culture, they better understand what culture is, and therefore have better insight into the differences between cultures.

Nonverbal Communication

Nonverbal communication is the communication that surrounds or replaces words. Nonverbal messages work with verbal messages to create meaning, or create a message that we mentally interpret with words.

A nonverbal message can *accent* what a word means, like an italic would in writing. Stressing one word, or looking angry while complaining about something, accents the meaning we are trying to convey.

Nonverbal communication can *complement* the words to clarify or reinforce the meaning of what is being said. We might shake our heads a certain way to support the meaning of a story we are telling about a business deal that went bad.

We might say certain words, yet *contradict* what we are saying with our nonverbal message. For example, we might use a sarcastic tone while saying how much we enjoy doing something.

We might *regulate* our message with our nonverbal cues. A drop in the voice and pause might indicate it is O.K. for another person to start speaking. As a teacher, I hate it when students start putting their books in their backpacks to send me a nonverbal message that class is over and I should stop speaking.

Nonverbal messages can also *substitute*, or replace, verbal messages. A nod to indicate yes, a V for victory sign, a smile of appreciation, are all substitutes for words. If we like someone, we might pat him or her on the top of the head to show approval. (Be careful! In Buddhist countries, the head is sacred, the center of spiritual as well as intellectual power, and should not be touched.)

Nonverbal communication can have *unintentional* as well as *intentional* meanings. Nonverbal messages may be misinterpreted. In Thailand, for instance, never point your toes at someone when sitting across from him or her. It is considered an insult, whether or not you mean it.

Culture and Nonverbal Communication

Some nonverbal communication messages are *universal* in that all cultures seem to communicate them in the same way. A shrug of the shoulders, for instance, means the same thing in virtually every culture. Certain facial expressions indicate a specific emotion, perhaps signifying a genetic or biological basis. Most of the nonverbal messages we see, hear, smell, and feel, however, are *culture specific,* which makes communicating between cultures difficult.

It is not within the scope of this book to explain all types of nonverbal messages. Below we review different types of nonverbal messages to gain a better understanding of what people might mean as they use them. At the least, we'll understand that they might mean something different from what we assume. Differences in nonverbal communication exist. Remain flexible and don't jump to conclusions (remember the Rolling the D.I.E. exercise from Chapter Three). The more we understand nonverbal communication, the better we communicate.

Types of Nonverbal Communication

One way to understand nonverbal communication is to understand the different types that exist.

Body Language. Body language is perhaps the best-known form of nonverbal communication. It includes how we communicate with our whole bodies as well as our hand gestures, facial expressions, and eye movements.

We communicate in many ways with our bodies. Our *posture* often communicates our attentiveness. In mainstream American culture, it is acceptable to stand with hands on hips. In many Asian cultures, such a posture would be considered an attempt to intimidate. The way a Japanese businessperson bows has a very specific meaning. A specific way of walking across a room might exhibit confidence in one culture and cockiness in another.

Gestures can have very specific meanings, and tend to be very culture specific. One culture's sign for hello might be another culture's sign of extreme contempt. Pointing with an index finger is an acceptable gesture for directing somebody's attention in one culture, while it is impolite in another, and so rude in another that it might cause a fight.

Facial expressions, as noted above, can be universal, but not all of them are. Something as innocent as a smile can cause major problems in the workplace. One person's smile might indicate a lack of seriousness, while another's may cover up anger, and a third might cover embarrassment.

Eye communication also varies from culture to culture. We communicate attention, interest, and many other things with our eyes. Sustained eye contact with a superior could mean respect and attentiveness in one culture, aggression in another, and disrespect in a third. Avoiding eye contact can mean dishonesty, modesty, or respect depending on the cultural setting.

Touch. Touch is a human being's first sensation. It is also our first communication. The way a parent touches his child helps the child develop a world view. An American businessperson firmly gripping a hand during a handshake communicates a sense of confidence and power. Women tend to hug more than men in the American business community. Scandinavians may be considered cold by some cultures, because they rarely touch another person in a public or business setting. People raised in Southern European cultures tend to touch more than people raised in Northern European cultures.

Smell. Many people don't realize the extent to which smell is a form of communication. Whether it is the perfume or aftershave a person wears to create a certain attraction, or an incense a southern Asian burns to create a spiritual effect, we knowingly (and unknowingly) communicate with odors.

Artifacts. Everything we do as humans communicates a message to the people around us. The cars we drive, the houses we live in, and the clothes and jewelry we wear all tell the world a little bit about who we are. Dressing for success—whatever the particular cultural style—is a universal nonverbal communication concept. In Japan, wearing a very expensive blazer and slacks is considered bad form; unmatched business attire is communicating too casual an image. On the other hand, some organizational cultures in the United States today are very casual, or have a weekly "casual day." International colleagues who come to those organizations on those days may be shocked, and find it difficult to do business.

Use of Space. We all use space differently. In southern Europe and northern Africa, people hold public conversations practically touching each other. Northern Europeans tend to shy away from such closeness. An African worker tells the story of his first days in the United States. He boarded a bus late one evening and noticed only one person on the bus. In his culture he would have been considered rude and unsociable to sit anywhere but right next to the other passenger. The person he sat next to, a small white woman, complained to the bus driver that the large black man was harassing her. Similarly, many difficulties can arise in the workplace because one person doesn't understand another person's sense of space.

Use of Time. Use of time is culturally based and varies from culture to culture. In the mainstream culture in the United States, we expect exactness of time. We feel it is rude if someone is late. "Time is money" is a common expression. In other cultures, time is more elastic and relative. Time spent on enjoyment and in relationships is more highly valued than it is in the United States.

Paralanguage. Paralanguage is all of the things that give emphasis and meaning to the words a person uses. It is the tone of voice, volume, rate of speed, use of pauses, rhythm, pitch, inflections, stresses, and other vocal sounds surrounding speech (including sighs, giggles, and groans). We put a lot of stock in how a person says the words she or he speaks. People in U.S. organizations who speak softly often feel overlooked. A monotone might seem to indicate disinterest, though it might not mean that at all. We've all heard the joke that certain people can read a telephone directory aloud and make it sound interesting, while others can read the most emotional writing imaginable and put an audience to sleep.

Different Communication Styles

What we say and how we say it, including the silent messages of nonverbal signals, are learned as part of our cultural upbringing. These communication preferences and habits can often seem "right" to us, while the communication styles of other cultures may seem strange or even repugnant. Social distance during conversation is an example. Two Americans in conversation will typically choose to separate themselves by a matter of three feet or more. In France or Italy, however, that distance may shrink to less than two feet. Is one culture right and the other wrong? Of course not. But we may nevertheless feel discomfort when our communication style conflicts with that of another culture.

The key is to prevent such discomfort from becoming an unexamined prejudice. The chart in Exhibit 4.3, adapted from *Managing Diversity*, by Gardenschwartz and Rowe,[5] can help us call to a conscious level those cultural differences. By recognizing these differences, we can avoid the pitfalls of bias and prejudice.

EXHIBIT 4.3
TYPES OF STYLE DIFFERENCES

Aspects of Culture	Mainstream American Culture	Different Cultures
Communication and Language	Explicit, direct communication	Implicit, indirect communication
	Emphasis on content—meaning found in words	Emphasis on context—meaning found around words
Food and Eating Habits	Eating as a necessity—fast food	Dining as a social experience
		Religious rules
Relationships, Family, Friends	Focus on nuclear family	Focus on extended family
	Responsibility for self	Loyalty and responsibility to family
	Value on youth, age seen as handicap	
		Age given status and respect

(Continued)

EXHIBIT 4.3
TYPES OF STYLE DIFFERENCES *(Concluded)*

Aspects of Culture	Mainstream American Culture	Other Cultures
Values and Norms	Individual orientation	Group orientation
	Independence	Conformity
	Preference for direct confrontation of conflict	Preference for harmony
Beliefs and Attitudes	Egalitarian	Hierarchical
	Challenging of authority	Respect for authority and social order
	Individuals control their destiny	Individuals accept their destiny
	Gender equity	Different roles for men and women
Mental Processes and Learning Style	Linear, logical, sequential	Lateral, holistic, simultaneous
	Problem-solving focus	Accepting of life's difficulties
Work Habits and Practices	Emphasis on task	Emphasis on relationships
	Rewards based on individual achievement	Rewards based on seniority, relationships
	Work has intrinsic value	Work is a necessity of life

Source: Adapted from Lee Gardenschwartz and Anita Rowe, *Managing Diversity* (New York: Irwin Professional Publishing, 1993).

Gender Differences in Communication

Even within a culture, strong differences in communication styles can be observed. In mainstream U.S. culture, for example, men and women are socialized to communicate in strikingly different ways.

American Men. Many American men traditionally have been socialized to see the world as a place where the individual establishes and protects his territory. They see life as a competition to win or lose. They have been taught to either stand up for themselves or face being called "cry-baby," "sissy," or worse. From early childhood through adulthood, they play win/lose games, including war games and athletic competitions. Some of these games involve teamwork, yet even then the role of the individual is emphasized. Robert Bly claims most American men lack the ability to have what he calls a "soul union," an intimate male friend, because we have been improperly initiated by older males and don't know ourselves properly. American men tend to view communication in individualistic win/lose terms. Communication is often like a game to prove superiority or domination, to maintain independence, and to avoid failure.

American Women. Many American women traditionally have been socialized to see the world as a place where the individual is a part of a community and to see life as an effort to maintain closeness with the community. They have been taught the importance of their physical appearance as well as the restrictions placed on them in the name of "protection." Women are often encouraged to think of themselves in relationship to others rather than as independently defined persons. As a result, women tend to view communication in terms of cooperation with others. Communication is often a way to seek confirmation and support, and to maintain connections.

Masculine and Feminine Speaking Styles

If you look at the styles created by American society as a continuum, the following examples of masculine and feminine speaking styles represent ends of the continuum. By understanding speaking styles, we understand better how to listen to people with those styles.

Masculine Speaking Style. The American masculine style is to speak in public (studies have shown that even women teachers call on boys more than girls, which helps lead to this), but not in private—(what Debra Tannen calls report versus rapport).[6] Men also tend to be competitive in speech to prove they are the best. They interrupt more often, and they exaggerate. Men tend to be "bottom line," or linear in their logic, and direct.

Feminine Speaking Style. American women tend to be more comfortable with an interpersonal speaking style. They ask questions, and seek unity and consensus in their speech. They use more qualifying phrases, tag-on comments, and deference. They also can speak in more than one conversation at the same time, what is called "simultaneous speech." Their communication tends to be indirect.

Julia Wood created the chart in Exhibit 4.4, which gives a slightly different slant on masculine and feminine speaking styles.[7]

Other Communication Style Differences

Socialization also creates other differences that affect communication styles. Our socialization depends upon when and where we were raised. People of different ages will have differences in their styles.

Socialization affects gays and lesbians because of what our society says about who they are. They have developed their own styles in response to that socialization.

For people with disabilities, both the socialization and the nature of the disability affect their style. Nonverbal communication is different when someone cannot walk or move his or her hands, or speaks with slurred speech. The following are specific styles of communication among the deaf who use American Sign Language:

- Their first language is American Sign Language.

EXHIBIT 4.4
MASCULINE AND FEMININE SPEAKING STYLES

Masculine Talk

1. Use talk to assert yourself and your ideas.

2. Personal disclosures can make you vulnerable.

3. Use talk to establish your status and power.

4. Matching experiences is a competitive strategy to command attention.

5. To support others, do something helpful—give advice or solve a problem for them.

6. Don't share the talk stage with others; interrupt others to make your point.

7. Each person is on his or her own in conversations, responsible for being heard.

8. Use responses to make your own points and outshine others.

9. Be assertive so others perceive you as confident and in command.

10. Talking should convey information and accomplish goals; extraneous details get in the way and don't achieve anything.

Feminine Talk

1. Use talk to build and sustain rapport with others.

2. Share yourself and learn about others by disclosing.

3. Use talk to create symmetry/equality between people.

4. Matching experiences with others shows understanding and empathy.

5. To support others, express understanding of their feelings.

6. Include others in conversation by asking questions and encouraging them to elaborate.

7. Keep the conversation going by asking questions and expressing interest in others' ideas.

8. Be responsive; let others know you care about what they say.

9. Be tentative so that others feel free to add their ideas.

10. Talking enhances relationships; details and interesting side comments increase the depth of connection.

- Deaf people also write notes to people who aren't deaf, or use a TTD, or send e-mail.

- Lip reading is not reliable (only 30 percent of English is readable on lips).

- Group solidarity is a strong value among deaf people.

- Deaf people tend to communicate in a narrative rather than episodic style. In other words, they start at the beginning and communicate in chronological order.

Many of these styles can affect communication in the workplace. Deaf people commonly complain that they are not understood, largely because people who can hear have no patience for their differences in style.

Learning Specific Style Differences

At times it becomes imperative to understand another's background in order to improve communication. If a specific group of people with cultural or other differences is having difficulties in your workplace, the best thing may be to study that group's culture or difference. Once you have a thorough knowledge of why people are behaving a certain way, you, as an executive, can help them and the people communicating with them create a better workplace environment.

Diversity Tips

1. Respect and appreciation for differences in communication style, background, and values enhance workplace communication.

2. It may be necessary to tolerate what is not easy to understand.

3. Flexibility in adapting to new communication situations is a valuable asset.

4. Constantly working on listening skills leads to better communication.

5. Understanding the obstacles to effective listening helps to overcome them.

6. Active Listening encourages and clarifies communication.

7. Empathy, or trying to feel what the speaker is feeling, aids in interpreting communication.

8. Learning to read nonverbal communication increases understanding.

9. Learning specific style differences can be crucial, especially when you communicate with a certain group a great deal.

5

Effective Communication in a Diverse Organization

The simple act of recognizing diversity in corporate life helps us to connect the great variety of gifts that people bring to the work and service of the organization.

Max DePree
Leadership Is an Art [1]

O ver a one-year period, the composition of the Board of Directors of a nonprofit charitable organization changed from homogeneous to diverse. New board members included an Asian woman, a blind man, and an Apache man. Ramona, the President of the Board, opened the first Board meeting by welcoming the new members and having everyone talk a little about their backgrounds.

Ramona noticed, though, that one Board member who had always been extremely open seemed less forthcoming at this meeting. He told Ramona he felt that the new members changed the dynamics of the group. Another member called Ramona, concerned that the Asian woman didn't speak up enough, and wondered if she was a good Board choice. The two new men also approached Ramona. They felt that the older members of the Board were too accommodating, and questioned people's sincerity. Ramona explained to each of these members that things might be a little uneasy at first, and asked them to give it some time.

To be an effective communicator, Ramona must understand the needs of the different people on the Board, and understand that their different styles might complicate the functioning of the Board. She must communicate to and facilitate the group in such a way that it is able to come together and be effective.

Below are the ten techniques for effective communication in a diverse workplace we will explore in this chapter:

- Be Open
- Listen effectively
- Communicate Empathy
- Use Inclusive language
- Speak with a sense of Equality
- Be Supportive
- Exhibit Confidence
- Be Other-oriented
- Be Flexible
- Metacommunicate

BE OPEN

When people feel free to talk, they will talk. Perhaps nothing helps good communication more than an open environment. Sharing a part of yourself tends to open up other people to you. Be open to the differences that exist among people. Effective communicators know that by sharing a part of themselves and helping others do the same, they create an open environment.

Being open implies that a communicator is open to understanding differences in people. An open communicator also accepts responsibility for the communication. For example, rather than saying "Your ethnic jokes are offensive," an open communicator might say, "I am offended by your ethnic jokes." The person telling the jokes now understands he or she is disturbing you, rather than wondering who is offended, who you are speaking for, and what you mean by "offensive." (We explore "I" statements in fuller detail in Chapter Seven.)

Self-Disclosure

The more open we are, the more we communicate. One of the most important aspects of open communication is self-disclosure. By sharing parts of our lives, we enable others to open themselves and share parts of their lives with us. The result is greater trust.

If we can be open about ourselves, our cultures, and the problems we see because of our differences, we have established a constructive starting point for more effective communication and better understanding.

Taking Responsibility

Imagine someone stepping forward and saying, "I want us to understand each other better because we need to work together." That person's use of an "I" statement shows she is taking responsibility for her role in any misunderstanding. She then reveals a few things about herself, about why her culture prevents her from accepting a certain type of behavior. The rest of the people she is talking with now are able to understand why she is having problems. They understand the need to communicate to her the reasons for their behavior. Problem solving has begun because one person has, by being open, taken on a leadership role.

LISTEN EFFECTIVELY

Listening might be the most important communication skill. Opening ourselves to communication implies that we need to listen to what others say. Listen actively to be sure you understand what is being communicated. Listen proactively to assure that you come away from the communication with the information you need.

Proactive Listening

We use Proactive Listening to discover the information we are looking for or that we feel should be openly discussed. Proactive listening gives the listener more control of the communication, something that can be extremely important to a leader. When we practice Proactive Listening, we listen, interpret, and ask questions to move the communication forward.

The goals of Proactive Listening include:

- To get the information that you, as a listener, need to know: The speaker doesn't always know what information needs to be communicated. A good listener, one who asks questions to direct the speaker to the areas that need to be discussed, makes a good executive and leader.

- To direct the speaker to ensure that the speaker is communicating what is intended: A speaker might believe he is communicating what he intends to say, but he may need help. A good proactive listener can help direct the speaker to say what he really wants to say by directing him with questions.

- To delve deeper into a topic than the speaker might go on his own: A speaker might not understand that the listener needs more information. A speaker might even intend to hide some of the information. An effective proactive listener can probe the speaker with questions to elicit more information.

- To help the speaker fully explore his or her thoughts and feelings: The more an effective proactive listener asks questions to gather information, the more the speaker has a chance to reflect on what he or she is saying. The speaker comes away with a better understanding of her own thoughts and feelings.

- To assure that both speaker and listener get as much from the communication as is needed: The ultimate aim of good Proactive Listening is to assure that everyone understands each other. The speaker and the listener come away from the communication more fully satisfied, both feeling that they got what they needed from the communication.

Using Proactive Listening

The point of Proactive Listening is to analyze and interpret. A Proactive Listener needs both the ability to listen extremely well and the confidence to direct the communication to specific areas. The listener must strive to understand the person who is talking, to help him explore his thoughts in a fuller way than he might have without the listener's efforts, and to direct him to the information the listener thinks is important.

The best way to accomplish the Proactive Listening goals is to ask good open-ended questions that cannot be easily answered with a simple "yes" or "no." For instance, if a person says she is troubled by the gay bashing in the lunch room, ask what forms the gay bashing takes, how it makes the speaker feel and why, and what types of comments begin the gay bashing. As you listen, find the cues to the areas you feel need to be explored, and ask questions about what has been said.

Proactive Listening in a Diverse Organization

By listening carefully and understanding diversity issues (see Chapter Two), the leader may hear something that needs to be expanded on, clarified, or changed in a way that makes the situation more understandable. Proactive Listening facilitates exploration of the problems that might arise because of diversity.

Imagine a situation where an African American member of your team comes to you shaking with rage. He tells you another member of the team made racist remarks. He is too full of anger to fully tell you what happened. How well you listen and how you direct the communication will have a profound influence on how you solve the problem and get on with the work that needs to be done. You need to listen well enough to find what comments were said, and the environment in which they were made. You need to ask questions that will help you find the information you need. You need to help the employee calm down. Your concerns are with both the employee and the future of your team.

Practice is key to becoming an effective proactive listener. The types of exercises suggested for Active Listening in Chapter Four will also work with Proactive Listening.

COMMUNICATE EMPATHY

Both Active and Proactive Listening can help us empathize with another person. Empathy as a way to learn about others was discussed in Chapter Four. Once we think we understand what the other person might be feeling, it is important to communicate that empathy.

Tools for Communicating Empathy

Communicating empathy is a basic communication skill. One tool, or way to communicate empathy, is to put yourself in the position of a person from another background. Try to see the world from this different perspective. Communicate your understanding. Share with the other person similar experiences you have had. If you are working with someone new to this country, tell them about your experiences in other countries to show you can understand some of what they are experiencing.

Active Listening is another tool for communicating empathy. Paraphrasing back to a speaker what they said (and making sure to communicate what you perceive to be their feelings) shows you are truly interested in understanding them. You may want to skip the words they tell you and just paraphrase the emotions you feel. For example, "I sense you are angry at the situation."

Nonverbal Empathy

A nod of the head, a smile or frown, the use of eye contact or touch (where appropriate) can go a long way toward showing the speaker you are trying to empathize with him or her.

Communicating empathy helps create a good communication environment. It lets the speaker know that you care enough to be doing all you can to understand him or her. Empathy is particularly important in a diverse organization where people from a nondominant culture might feel ill-at-ease. A good leader helps everyone feel they can and will be heard.

WORDS, REALITIES, AND INCLUSIVE LANGUAGE

Language is powerful. We need to be very careful that we use language in ways that help people feel included. Inaccurate labels and noninclusive language make people feel disrespected and left out, regardless of whether the speaker intended any slight. How many girls never decided to join a police force because they couldn't become a "police *man*?" How many people from other countries have felt left out of the conversation because we consistently used baseball metaphors such as "three strikes and you're out"? It is important to think about and adjust our language to make it more effective for our listeners, especially when they come from backgrounds different from our own.

Gender and Language Suggestions

Below are several examples of how one can be more inclusive in gender communication.

1. Watch out for language that suggests that men are the standard human beings. For references to all human beings, use "people" or "humanity" instead of "man" or "mankind."

2. Do not use the masculine pronouns "he," "his," "him," or "himself" for a generic reference to individual men and women. Instead:

- Substitute the appropriate plural form: "they," "their," "them," or "themselves."

- Use "she or he," "him or her," and "himself or herself."

- Rephrase the sentence so that no singular pronoun is necessary. For example, instead of "the supervisor has weekly meetings with his staff," you could say, "the supervisor holds weekly staff meetings."

- Use alternating female and male examples.

3. Avoid using job titles that end in the suffix "man" or "men." Substitute descriptive and neutral titles, for example, "firefighter" for "fireman," "chair" for "chairman," or "mail carrier" for "mailman."

4. Avoid prefacing an occupational title with a reference to the person's gender, for example, "woman doctor," "male secretary," "male nurse," "female supervisor." It is usually irrelevant.

5. For terms where gender is irrelevant, substitute a descriptive, neutral term. For example, use "synthetic" for "man-made," or "flight attendant" for "stewardess."

6. Be consistent and parallel in your use of titles and first names, for example, "Senators Kennedy and Feinstein," not "Senator Kennedy and Dianne Feinstein" or "Kennedy and Mrs. Feinstein."

Inclusive Language and Empowerment

The only power some people have is the ability to name themselves. What we call people makes a difference to them. By calling them what they want to be called, we empower them, and help them feel a sense of worth. They have a sense of inclusion when they feel empowered.

Sexual Orientation. Most people feel, and authorities agree, that we determine our sexuality early in life and, as a rule, we cannot change it. Therefore, "sexual orientation" is a more accurate term to describe a person's sexuality than "sexual preference" or "choice." The clinical term "homosexual" may be appropriate in certain contexts, but generally the terms "gay men," "lesbians," and "gay people" are preferable.

We need to avoid the terms "lifestyle" or "alternative lifestyle" as euphemisms because gay men and lesbians, like heterosexuals, have a variety of lifestyles. Many people use the term "domestic partner" instead of "spouse" to refer to the person with whom one shares a household on a permanent basis, whether married or not.[2]

People with Disabilities. Below are some tips for communicating with people with disabilities.[3] When you meet a deaf or hearing-impaired person:

- Face the person directly, and on the same level whenever possible.
- Do not eat, chew, or smoke while talking because it makes your speech more difficult to understand.
- Keep your hands away from your face while talking.
- Reduce background noises when carrying on conversation—turn off radio and TV.
- Never talk from another room. Be sure to get the person's attention before you start speaking.
- Speak in a normal fashion without shouting. Be sure the light is not shining in the eyes of the person.
- If the person has difficulty understanding something, find a different way of saying the same thing, rather than repeating the original words over and over. Bring the person into a group conversation by describing briefly the topic you are discussing.
- If the person is using a sign language interpreter, remember to look at the hearing-impaired or deaf person while you talk, not the interpreter, so the person can see your facial expressions.

When you meet a blind or visually impaired person:

- Be sure to tell the person who you are when you enter a room where a blind person is. Tell the person when you leave so that she is not left talking to an empty room.

- Talk directly to the person who is severely visually impaired, not the person's companion. Loss of sight does not affect a person's mental ability. Also, there is no need to shout; sight and hearing ability are not related.

- Don't be afraid to use words like "see" and "look" because they are an integral part of our language. People who are blind use them all the time.

- In a restaurant, offer to read the menu for the person who is visually impaired, but let the person order his or her own meal. Also, it's very helpful to a blind person if you describe where items are placed on the table.

- Walking with a person who is visually impaired, let the person take your arm just above the elbow. Allow the person to walk a step behind you so that it will be easy to follow the motion of your body. Pause briefly before steps and curbs and tell the person what is ahead.

- If you are guiding a person who is visually impaired to be seated, simply place the individual's hand on the back of the chair and let the person take over from there.

When you meet a mobility impaired person:

- Offer to help when it looks as though it might be needed, but do not insist on it if the person declines aid. If help is wanted, ask, "How can I help?"

- Don't hover. Adults with disabilities do not wish to be treated like babies or as incompetents. Everyone

should be given the opportunity to make indepen-
dent decisions.

- When a person with a disability falls, take it easy.
Wait for a cue. The person may prefer to get up
without help and will indicate to you if help is
necessary.

- Don't take crutches and wheelchairs away from a
person with a disability unless that person prefers to
have them out of the way. These are necessary
accessories for some people.

- Let the individual tell you how to help. Steps can
be difficult to navigate even for the young and
agile. Some people with a disability may need help.
Those who do not need to be helped usually have
methods of their own for negotiating steps. Do not
pull an arm or push from behind unless such
assistance has been requested. Precarious balance
can be lost entirely with such tactics.

- Always ask before offering assistance, for example,
to a person on crutches who is going through a
doorway. If the door is being used as a means of
support, you could accidentally cause the person to
fall by opening the door too soon.

- Remember that most wheelchair users are not
confined to their wheelchairs. Some can walk to a
limited extent, and others frequently transfer in and
out of their chairs by using the strength in their
arms.

When you meet a speech-impaired person:

- Try to find a place where the noise level is low, so
the conversation will have as little competition as
possible.

- Try not to pretend to understand what the person is
saying when you do not. Nod your head "yes" only
if you understood the message.

- Do not be concerned about asking the person to repeat the message. A speech-impaired person is aware that his or her speech may be difficult to understand and can often use different words to express the same idea.

- Try to relax and listen. Do not finish the person's sentence. You may have the wrong idea, and this can be frustrating for both people.

- Don't be afraid to communicate with someone with a speech problem. The more you communicate together, the easier it will become for you to understand each other.

Stereotypes and Exclusion

People often define themselves by their gender, race/ethnicity, sexual orientation, nation of origin, age, disability, class, and religion. We have to be careful, however, not to refer to an individual as a member of his group unless specifically relevant to the topic being discussed. We limit a person by defining him by what group he is a member of rather than by who he is as an individual, and by what he has accomplished. Stereotypes become dangerous when fixed generalizations about a group negatively influence our perceptions of an individual.

Other than for specific reasons (e.g., performing in a youth symphony) mentioning age merely sets up expectations that need not be created. Similarly, religion, race, cultural background, class: none of these things has anything to do with a person's job. Referring to people by these group designations only gives impertinent information that may affect others' perceptions of their performance. Not referring to people by their specific background includes them as part of an organization and community.

Metaphors, Idioms, and Exclusion

Executives can inspire their employees with good visual metaphors, yet the strength of metaphors can also be their weakness.

When a metaphor creates a clear image, it is one of the strongest forms of speech. But when the symbol is unclear—as is sometimes the case when communicating with people from different backgrounds—the image often creates confusion. In such situations, people from different backgrounds are left out, excluded from the communication.

For instance, sports metaphors, which are ubiquitous in American speech, often leave the uninitiated out of the discussion. For people who understand football, the image of "making a goal line stand"—stopping the adversary from scoring— indicates winning a competition against the odds. It's a powerful metaphor. But to a person who has never watched football, the use of the expression "We'll have to make a goal line stand" is meaningless. Using the image to refer to preventing a hostile takeover implies that we need to do everything we can to stop the takeover. Anyone not familiar with football will not understand the metaphor and will be excluded from the conversation.

The same is true for military metaphors. Metaphors can be used to get people to think about what we say. But when a metaphor cannot be understood, it leaves people out.

Idioms or figures of speech peculiar to a particular people or region are similar to metaphors in how they affect listeners. Idioms are like a code; they can be colorful and descriptive, but the listener must know the idiom to understand what the speaker is saying. They are exclusive.

SPEAK WITH A SENSE OF EQUALITY

Talking to people in an organization as they talk to each other, or as you would talk to your peers, helps create a sense of equality. There are several keys to speaking with a sense of equality.

- Don't lecture. Let everyone have an equal opportunity to speak.
- Try not to demand. Make polite requests such as "Would you please take this report to the marketing manager?"

- Avoid using phrases that indicate inequality, such as "You should write that letter."
- Don't constantly correct the other person. By correcting him or her you are stressing your superiority.
- Praise the other person for what he or she contributes. Communicate your respect.
- Monitor your nonverbal cues. It is important, in American culture, to have good eye contact, to smile and nod your head in approval, and to do other things that show both respect and approval.

Hewlett-Packard is an organization that both embraces diversity and asks its managers to communicate to the organization's diverse workforce in substantive and innovative ways. All H-P managers must take a multi-day Managing Diversity course. They must also go out into the workforce and talk not only with their own subordinates, but to a wide variety of other H-P employees as well. H-P uses its variation of the Tom Peters system of Managing by Walking Around (MBWA). Managers must spend a certain amount of time each week walking around their workplaces, talking with individuals and groups. As they walk around, they constantly work on their skills in effective communication.

Achieving a sense of equality in our communication is an important executive skill in a diverse workplace. People will be less concerned about differences when they feel like members of a team with shared goals.

BE SUPPORTIVE

Be supportive of the ways other people do things. Try not to be judgmental or certain that your way is the only way. Be positive rather than negative. Positive interpersonal relationships are built by people communicating in such a way that their relationship is supported, validated, and enhanced by the communication. An executive gets the most out of the people she works with in part because of the respect shown for the diversity of styles and willingness to hear opposing points of view. A diverse workforce is full of new ideas and different approaches to traditional methods. Supporting people in their attempts to find new ways of doing things benefits everyone.

Richard Notebaert, Chairman of Ameritech, actively communicates his communication skills on many levels. One of the main mechanisms the organization uses to make diversity work is to empower advocacy groups. The company's Black Advocacy Panel, for example, reviews corporate policy on a wide variety of issues, including downsizing and Affirmative Action. It also works to improve diversity at top levels. In June 1995, the panel held a summit with 400 people, including Notebaert. The executive outlined company diversity strategies in such a way that one black employee commented: "I feel like there is someone standing up for me. It makes me feel better about Ameritech."[4]

Positive Strokes

People can be stroked with a smile, or an encouraging word. Leaders who stroke the people who work for them encourage them to continue working and putting in the effort to make the organization thrive. Another way of communicating support is by emphasizing the positive rather than the negative. Negative communication creates barriers to good communication and discourages people from doing their best job.

Supportive communication has the following attributes:[5]

1. Supportive communication is problem-oriented, not person-oriented. Say "How can we solve this problem?" rather than "Because of you there is a problem."

2. Supportive communication is congruent. Say "Your behavior really upset me" if this is the case, **Not** "Do I seem upset? No, everything's fine."

3. Supportive communication is descriptive, not evaluative. Say "Here is what happened; here is my reaction; here is what I suggest would be more acceptable to me" rather than starting out with "You are wrong for doing what you did."

4. Supportive communication is validating. "I have some ideas, but do you have any suggestions?" is more validating than "You wouldn't understand, so we'll do it my way."

5. Supportive communication is specific rather than global. Say, for example, "You interrupted me three times during the meeting" rather than "You're always trying to get attention."

6. Supportive communication is conjunctive. Saying "Relating to what you just said, I'd like to discuss this" is better than "I want to discuss this (regardless of what you want to discuss)."

7. Supportive communication is owned, not disowned. For example, "I've decided to turn down your request because . . ." is better than "You have a pretty good idea, but they just wouldn't approve it."

8. Supportive communication requires supportive listening. Say "What do you think are the obstacles standing in the way of improvement?" rather than "As I said before, you make too many mistakes. You're just not doing the job."

Exhibit Confidence

People need a sense of confidence to actively share in communication. A confident communicator can help create an environment where everyone is more confident. A confident communicator is relaxed, giving, and helpful to others, and does not fear what others bring to the communication. Display tolerance of differences by remaining confident and comfortable with yourself without being arrogant.

People often feel a lack of confidence when communicating with people from different cultures and backgrounds. They may not know the rules, or they might feel they are looked down upon by others. When you as a leader are perceived to be confident in your ideas, you model confidence for others around you.

Modeling confidence also improves employees' self-esteem. When people feel good about themselves, they feel good about the work they do. When everyone contributes, there is more innovation and higher productivity. Self-esteem can lead to conflict when people believe in their ideas and are confident in presenting and defending them, but this conflict can be managed to make it a positive rather than negative force. (Chapter Seven concentrates on managing conflict.)

BE OTHER-ORIENTED

Being other-oriented means you are interested in what others bring to the communication. Show your involvement in what others are saying. Let them speak. Help facilitate a good back and forth communication, where no one dominates.

An important skill in being other-oriented is communicating immediacy. Immediacy means being involved in the conversation as it takes place and not letting other things on your mind affect that conversation. Immediacy is a quality that many top executives have. They make each person feel like the most important person in their world at that moment. They empower and inspire employees with that sense. When communicating with a person whose background is different than yours, there is a good chance the person might be nervous, lack self-confidence, or be confused about the communication. By communicating immediacy, you break down the barriers to good communication.

A lot of immediacy is nonverbal. It is a sense that you are right with the other person in the conversation. Part of it is focusing your attention on the person. You might smile or nod your head. Perhaps you will touch the person or at least lean toward him (where culturally appropriate). Eye contact is also important, as long as it doesn't make the person uncomfortable.

You can also communicate immediacy verbally. When speaking to a person, try to use her name. Use the word "we" often to include her. Compliment and support her. Show that you have heard what she has said by paraphrasing it or by asking a question.

BE FLEXIBLE

Adjust your communication according to the feedback you receive. Learn from your mistakes. Perhaps no skill is more important, in leadership or in communicating in a diverse organization, than flexibility. Flexibility means having the ability to adjust to the situation you are in. It does not imply being wishy-washy or uncommitted. In a diverse organization, you need to expect the unexpected. Every situation is new, and requires new thought, new actions.

We need to allow others, and ourselves, to make mistakes. Communicating in a diverse organization is not easy. Allow people to learn from their mistakes.

We also need to be flexible in terms of how we behave with different people. It is possible that you will treat an elderly white man one way and a young Asian woman another way—for good reason. Of course, you need to treat them equitably, but the two people might communicate differently, and you need to be able to communicate appropriately with each of them. Using the D.I.E. model discussed in Chapter Four is one way to help yourself learn how to avoid responding immediately. This will give you a chance to be flexible.

Flexibility is the key to many of the other skills noted in this chapter, as well as to good executive communication in a diverse organization. Executives who are willing to change position to enable workers to give their best efforts and who accept the many differences within the workforce can use those differences for the betterment of the organization.

METACOMMUNICATE

One of the most important tools a communicator has, especially in a diverse organization, is metacommunication. Metacommunication is communication about communication.

When people in an organization use different communication styles, it is extremely important to talk *about* the talk to make sure people understand each other. A woman from one culture may not show much emotion, for instance. When she tells you she appreciated your performance review, you might not sense she did. By talking about the communication, you make sure you understand what her feelings are.

Metacommunication can be verbal or nonverbal. You can say, "I want to be sure I understand what you are saying." You might also nonverbally look at the person to indicate that you are unsure of what he or she is communicating. Talking about the communication itself helps clarify our communication and helps us create shared meaning.

Diversity Tips

1. To encourage communication, be Open—share a part of yourself, and be open to the differences of others.

2. Both Active and Proactive Listening can be used to Listen effectively.

3. Empathy—communicating that you feel what the other feels—is key.

4. Inclusive language gives everyone access to the communication process.

5. Speak with a sense of Equality. People respond when they are respected as equals.

6. To be Supportive, accept the ways different people do things, validate both their efforts and who they are, and be positive.

7. Leaders who exhibit Confidence help others be confident and build self-esteem.

8. To be Other-oriented, show interest in what others bring to the communication process, and communicate a sense of immediacy.

9. Effective leaders are Flexible. They adjust to the differences people bring to communication.

10. Effective leaders Metacommunicate—they talk about the communication, to be sure everyone understands each other.

6

Diversity and Team-Building

Genuine leadership involves getting all the wisdom that is available in a group, and helping the group come to a better decision than any one of its members would have been able to achieve himself.

J. Irwin Miller[1]

Jane recently became the team leader of an engineering team. She immediately observed there was little interaction between the one gay male and two lesbian team members and the rest of the group. One team member, Fred, told Jane that he had heard two other team members cracking jokes about the gay team members over lunch. Fred felt that Ruth, in particular (whom he referred to as "a real bitch"), was creating tension and causing problems. He also

> felt another team member, Jason, was only
> going along with the gay bashing because "he
> wanted to go out with a white woman in the
> worst kind of a way."

Inattentive management created and fueled Jane's dysfunctional team. It suffers from sexism, racism, homophobia, and perhaps other problems. Teams are ubiquitous in today's organizational world. Executives are often team leaders and need to understand how to build, maintain, and nourish all of the members in their organizations.

A diverse work team can help its members understand the potential of diversity, and it can help successful employees in those teams gain stature in their organizations. Janie Payne, for example, orchestrated the most successful teams at Bell Atlantic Corp. Her first team was extremely successful. During her first two years on the team, customer response time was cut from eight days to eight hours, and the quality of service increased by more than 40 percent. Seven of fifteen members received promotions during that time. Payne and another colleague oversee Bell Atlantic's team initiatives for all of its 70,000 employees. She says the self-directed work team proves to be "the epitome of teams for empowering employees and encouraging them to appreciate the differences in the group."[2]

Standard Motor Products used to have major communications problems between its two blocks of employees, one consisting of African Americans and white employees, the other consisting of Asians and Latinos, many of whom did not speak English well. The language barrier led to other communication problems as well. The organization decided to create teams of employees with members from both blocks. The results: factory down time at Standard Motor Products has dropped 60 percent, and productivity has increased. Workers who had never spoken English in more than ten years with the company now do.[3]

USING THE TEAM-BUILDING WHEEL
TO CREATE A TEAM

The "Team-Building Wheel" in Exhibit 6.1 can be used to help create and maintain high-performance teams in a diverse workplace. Probably the best way to develop a team is to move clockwise around the Team-Building Wheel. The top spoke is Establish the Team's Mission, while the last spoke (moving counter clockwise) is Continuously Evaluate. All spokes are of equal importance, but some things need to be begun before others. A team must first get to know each other, establish a mission, and find ways to support each other. Evaluations obviously come after the team has been together a while. Developing a high-performance team is a continuous process.

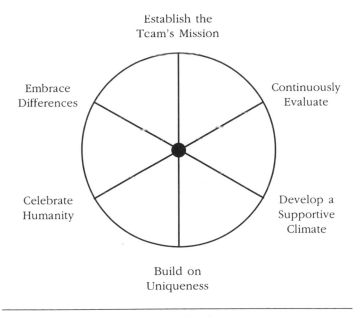

EXHIBIT 6.1
TEAM-BUILDING WHEEL

ESTABLISH THE TEAM'S MISSION

Finding, valuing, and using team members' unique talents develop how the team works together, but do little to focus the team on task. Just as an organization needs a mission to focus its goals and understand its core values and norms, a team also needs a mission. One of the most important roles of a group or team leader is to craft that mission and communicate it in ways to carry it out.

The nature of the team and the organization determine some of the team's mission. A marketing team in a computer software firm, for instance, needs to market the company's products to consumers and retail outlets, yet there are individual goals a team might determine for itself. Perhaps it wants to set a goal of the number of products to be sold that is higher than the organization's goal. Perhaps the team wants to use new media and new technologies, and create its own goals in those areas. A team might even create personal goals, concerning productivity, absenteeism, donations to charity, and so on.

Core Values

In order to fully understand its mission, a team must determine its core values. Some of these values will be typical team values (the meaning of working together, communication, respect for each other, tardiness and absenteeism norms, and so on). Diversity determines other core values. The following questions can help a team establish its core values:

- How important is our team's diversity?
- How can our diversity positively affect our team mission?
- How does our diversity affect our response to inevitable conflict?
- How do our individual values lead to different notions of what being a team member means?
- How do our differences in values shape each team member's acceptance and compliance with the team values?

- How does our diversity of values come together to form a single team's values?

Diversity issues are particularly important to the success or failure of the team. Team members from diverse backgrounds may have real differences in such areas as respect for authority, the meaning of the family and its effects on work, group versus individual emphasis, plus many verbal and nonverbal communication style differences that might make understanding the different values difficult. It is vital that the group members recognize each other's values and also move beyond recognition of individual values to find group norms that everyone can live with.

The Leader's Role in Developing a Meaningful Team Mission

There are several ways a leader can help a team determine a meaningful mission.

- The leader needs to get everyone involved in the process of creating and articulating the mission.
- The leader needs to keep the team focused on the mission and to keep it working well together to achieve its mission.
- The leader must continually inspire the team members to fulfill the mission. The leader can inspire with words and actions and model being a good team member.

Suggestions for Team Mission Creation

One of the best ways to create the team mission and to get all team members to buy into it is to have the team create it. The team leader should facilitate a discussion that includes all members. The discussion should cover specific areas such as team values, norms, and goals. Go through a process of finding agreement on each of these factors through consensus, not democratic vote. Each member needs to say he or she can live with the results.

Lead a discussion in each area, including a brainstorming session (see Exhibit 6.2) and an evaluative session. Keep these two sessions separate. Let team members brainstorm at will, then evaluate. Create a list, first of values, then norms, and finally goals. From this process, the team will arrive at the overall mission. Write out the team's mission statement and make sure the team has reached consensus on it.

EXHIBIT 6.2
BRAINSTORMING

Brainstorming works because it increases involvement and participation, produces a large number of ideas in a short time, and encourages creative thinking.

Brainstorming requires good facilitation skills by the team leader. She needs to keep team members focused on the topic and ideas, and not on personalities or on evaluating personal values.

Brainstorming Guidelines

1. Hold off on judgment.

2. Let the juices flow. Think of as many ideas as possible.

3. Piggyback.

4. No idea, no matter how stupid-sounding or unfeasible, is to be rejected.

5. Record all ideas.

6. Think about using turn-taking to get brainstorming started, but don't stick to it too long.

There should be absolutely no evaluations during brainstorming! The team leader needs to stop *any* comments about the feasibility of *any* idea.

Embrace Differences

We can be equal and still acknowledge our differences. Sweeping differences under the rug only leaves them there to surprise us at the worst moments. We *are* different. Only by learning about those differences can we utilize them to make our working relationships stronger and more effective.

Imagine a team that holds back minor prejudices. Some team members might not even realize they have any. Assumptions team members make about each others' work styles may lead to mistakes, which cause sloppy team performance. Assumptions may also lead to distrust and other personal problems, creating a dysfunctional team in which members don't work well together, and may even sabotage each others' work. Production goes down, and quality suffers.

Embracing differences does not mean that all differences are acceptable. Just as some behaviors and values are detrimental to an organization, some behaviors and values will hurt a team. Yet we need to discover those differences, acknowledge their existence, and learn how to best utilize whichever ones we can to create a good team.

Group Discussion Exercise

An effective leader facilitates discovery of differences. One way to begin the process of discovery is to conduct group Active Listening exercises. Another way is to facilitate a team discussion about differences. Make it fun. Perhaps kick the discussion off with one of the following questions.

- Think about where you lived when growing up. How did that influence who you are now?
- What specific aspect of your culture do you most appreciate and are not likely to give up?
- What do you remember most about your favorite holiday or tradition as you were growing up?

Valuing the Differences

A leader of a team helps the other members see reasons for valuing differences. For example, if a Latina comes up with an idea on a way to sell paper towels to the Latino/Latina community, the leader can let other members know it was her unique perspective that enabled the team to succeed.

A leader also models valuing differences by being flexible to change and letting the team have a good amount of control over its destiny. As a leader, if you have an idea of how to design a piece of software, but other team members suggest a different method, let them try their method. Help develop trust. A team that trusts its leader, and a leader who shows trust in his or her team, will be a successful team.

Reward the team's successes in a way that emphasizes the team's diversity. Facilitate a discussion to determine how the team wants to be rewarded. Discovering and valuing differences will help a team work together. The more we know about each other, the more we understand each other, the more we value each other, the better we communicate. An effective executive understands the need for her organization's teams to communicate well to work together successfully.

CELEBRATE HUMANITY

No matter how different we are from one another, we have more commonalities than differences. As human beings, we use language to communicate, and we are physiologically, genetically, and psychologically similar. We tend to love our children, enjoy play, and like food. Team members have more in common: they work for the same organization in the same location with the same people. Any good team discovers commonalities and builds on them. Commonalities show us we are together from the start and also give us a starting point to build from to become stronger.

A group Active Listening exercise can be a good team builder to help teams recognize similarities as well as discover differences. The group discussion exercise above will also bring out similarities as well as differences. A team leader may want to facilitate the discussion afterwards to emphasize the similarities or the differences discovered, or she might look at *both* at the same time.

The exercise in Exhibit 6.3, developed by Gardenschwartz and Rowe, can also be used for discovering both commonalities and differences.[4]

EXHIBIT 6.3
CROSS-CULTURAL TEAM-BUILDING SCALE

DIRECTIONS: For each item, each team member marks an X along the continuum to indicate his or her style preference.

Value change ———————+———————	Value tradition
Specificity in communicating	Vagueness in communicating
Analytical, linear problem solving	Intuitive, lateral problem solving
Emphasis on individual performance	Emphasis on group performance
Communication primarily verbal	Communication primarily nonverbal
Emphasis on task and product	Emphasis on relationship and process
Surface different views ———————+———————	Harmony
More horizontal organization	More vertical organization
Informal tone ———————+———————	Formal Tone
Competition ———————+———————	Collaboration
Rigid adherence to time	Flexible adherence to time

(Continued)

EXHIBIT 6.3
CROSS-CULTURAL TEAM-BUILDING SCALE *(Concluded)*

Once each team member has completed the chart, you can facilitate the exercise in several ways.

Option 1: Have each team member connect the Xs, and then compare each other's profiles.

Option 2: Place the charts side by side on a long table and compare them.

Option 3: Print the chart on transparencies so they can be overlaid. The graphics will either line up or be shown to be quite different, giving you starting points for discussion on differences and commonalities.

Option 4: Break the group into dyads and have the two people compare charts. Keep changing the dyads until everyone has had a chance to compare charts and discuss their differences and commonalities. Then facilitate a large group discussion about how different or similar the members of your team are.

Option 5: Clear an area of a room and draw an imaginary line. For each area on the chart, have people stand where they put their X on the continuum. People have fun doing this exercise, and it gets them moving. The fun and graphic nature of this form of viewing results always leads to a lively discussion.

Source: Adapted from Lee Gardenschwartz and Anita Rowe, *Managing Diversity* (New York: Irwin Professional Publishing, 1993).

BUILD ON UNIQUENESS

Even though we all have much in common, each of us is unique. We all bring individual strengths and styles to the workplace. A good team leader can get the most out of her team by building on the strengths and styles of each team member. By understanding each member's uniqueness, utilizing their strengths, and avoiding their weaknesses, the team achieves synergy, where the total is greater than the sum of its individual parts.

Finding Appropriate Tasks for Team Members

When a team leader assigns individual team members tasks they do best, they have the best chance for success. With success comes self-esteem. They will also feel good about the leader for acknowledging their skills. The leader builds trust. In general, people who feel their strengths are recognized and appreciated work harder and do a better job. When everyone feels good about being a member of the team, the team can enjoy working together and achieve a high performance level.

On a diverse team, it is especially important to find the tasks each individual handles best. Communication style differences might make one person qualified for the task of disseminating information. Another person might be from a culture that emphasizes the group over the individual and would be best suited for tasks more group than individual oriented. An individualist could be given tasks that don't require her to constantly interact with other group members. The team leader should find not only what the team member does well, but how that person communicates and what other individual and cultural traits might make that person best suited for specific tasks.

Equal Does Not Mean the Same

People work together well when they feel the team uses their talents well and treats them fairly. Teams often make the mistake of confusing fairness with treating people the same.

Here's an example. A design team believed equality was the most important team value and thought equality meant that everyone did every task. This talented team was not producing as much as other teams in the company, and the company's executives called a consultant in to work with them.

One of the consultant's first discoveries was that one team member did not like communicating team status to the vice president in charge of their division. The man had a thick accent and was self-conscious about his English. He knew that it would be his turn to make the next report for a month ahead of time, and for that entire month, he was unable to design. His nervousness harmed his creativity.

Through individual interviews, the consultant discovered other, similar problems on this team. After compiling a list of strengths and style differences, the whole team met and discussed the list. The team decided that equality was still important, but that utilizing each other's strengths need not mean unequal work loads or value to the team. The team became the top-producing design group in the organization within a year.

Interviewing Group Members to Assure Success

Individual interviews and a group meeting follow-up is a good way to discover and utilize each team member's talents and create a high-performance team. A team leader can do this type of interview and team meeting when she forms the team. The team leader can also keep tabs on how people are doing their tasks, and adjust the jobs each person does as necessary. Sometimes, though, it takes someone from outside the team to help, somebody with psychological distance, like the consultant in the above example. Another approach is to go outside the organization for a team-building activity.

Ropes Courses to Build and Maintain Diverse Teams

Ropes courses are excellent team-building activities and can help a team discover its differences and commonalities. Most of all, a ropes course can help a team discover and utilize the individual talents of each team member and get that team working together.

Standard ropes courses take teams outdoors and put the members through a series of exercises emphasizing most of the standard team-building concepts: establishing trust, getting the most out of each individual, finding how people can best mesh their talents, improving communication. Ropes courses can also be great devices for building and maintaining diverse teams, though the impact of diversity requires adjustments. Some ropes course providers include a debriefing on diversity or have a ropes course designed with diversity in mind.

DEVELOP A SUPPORTIVE CLIMATE

A team with members from diverse backgrounds will not last long, even with a good mission statement, if its members do not support each other. Diversity can cause a lack of confidence. A diverse team needs members to respect each other, praise each other, "stroke" each other for being the unique individual each team member is. The team leader needs to develop a supportive climate, model being supportive, facilitate support, and encourage it.

There are different ways to show support. Team members need to feel respected, safe, and that it is all right to make mistakes. They also should feel supported enough to be able both to give and receive constructive criticism (see "Giving Feedback" section below). Team members need to have flexibility in communication situations to show tolerance for different ways of doing things, and to recognize and validate each other's accomplishments.

The Function of a Supportive Climate

The following example demonstrates the need for a supportive climate and suggests ways to establish one.

An accounting team needs to send its superior the results of an audit. Ricardo, the team member chosen to do the job, is confused. The team has given him three sets of results, yet he knows only one set is the correct one. In Ricardo's culture, however, superiors want to review all team output, so Ricardo decides to send all three sets of results. This results in a bad evaluation from the superior, who only wanted one set. In a situation like this, Ricardo's team members must be flexible enough not to become upset. They need to understand why Ricardo made the mistake and that his confusion was based on style and behavioral differences. They should be critical of Ricardo only enough to help him so he won't make the same mistake again. The next time Ricardo is assigned a similar task, and does it well, the team should recognize and validate his accomplishment.

Equality, Support, Fun

A team with a sense of equality has a supportive climate. A sense of equality helps people feel they are an essential part of the team. A team member who feels equal will offer more opinions and take more risks. Team equality encourages cultural sensitivity and cultural equality.

A team also creates a supportive climate when its members help each other increase self-esteem and a sense of belonging. When people feel good about themselves and feel they belong on the team, they work together better.

They also work together better when they have fun. It is important for team members to see each other outside the normal work environment. Getting to know each other in a non-work environment helps in their teamwork on the job. Fun activities can range from team picnics to forming a recreational league volleyball team. The team could plan nights at a jazz club or monthly dinners, anything to get the team having fun together outside of work. Some teams go on outdoor retreats. Some of these retreats might be peaceful communing-with-nature geta-ways, while others might be challenging whitewater raft trips. These types of activities provide new experiences that often translate into greater understanding.

CONTINUOUSLY EVALUATE

Continuous process improvement has been one of the key rea-sons for the productivity successes of leading-edge companies in recent years. The best way a team can change is for team members to communicate and give each other feedback on a regular basis. Thus, change comes as a normal part of the team's growth and development. The team leader continuously evalu-ates, gives feedback, and develops mechanisms for fuller evalu-ations. The team should continuously evaluate its outcomes, and whether it is accomplishing its mission. Team-building exercises, done on a regular basis, will facilitate growth. A good team never stops growing, never stops communicating.

Giving Feedback

Immediate feedback will keep a team moving ahead. People should understand what they've been doing and how they've been working together. When the team does an evaluation, there should be no surprises. A leader can inspire and encourage team members to give each other feedback. It is vital that all team members feel comfortable enough to both give and receive feedback.

A leader can also encourage individual feedback through modeling. Use "I" statements (see Chapter Seven for more detailed discussion of "I" statements) to take ownership of the communication, so the person getting the feedback understands that the comments you make are your perceptions. "I" statements reduce defensiveness because they are not accusatory. Say things like, "I feel we need to work on our relationship" and "I've noticed the team doesn't function as well when we start work at different times." Avoid using the word "you," which sounds accusatory. It is always a good idea to end your "I" statement feedback by offering specific expectations for the future, such as "I would prefer us to find a time we can all agree on to start work."

Giving Constructive Criticism

"I" statements are effective, but they are only one aspect of giving constructive criticism. Good constructive criticism helps people learn how, and in what areas, they can improve. Constructive criticism motivates people and helps them by giving specific advice. Exhibit 6.4 offers advice on how to give good constructive criticism.

EXHIBIT 6.4
CONSTRUCTIVE CRITICISM FEEDBACK

INSTRUCTIONS: To evaluate your use of constructive criticism, respond to each question using the following scale:

1 = always; 2 = frequently; 3 = sometimes; 4 = seldom; 5 = never

_____ 1. Do you think through what you are going to say before saying it?

_____ 2. Do you focus primarily on what is done well?

_____ 3. Do you approach negatives in a constructive and concrete way, avoiding generalities?

_____ 4. Do you offer ways to improve?

(Continued)

EXHIBIT 6.4
CONSTRUCTIVE CRITICISM FEEDBACK *(Concluded)*

_____ 5. Do you criticize the speaker's message or behavior and not her or him?

_____ 6. Do you try to understand before you criticize?

_____ 7. Do you check your emotions before you criticize?

_____ 8. Do you check your biases before you criticize?

_____ 9. Do you avoid over-honesty and frankness?

_____ 10. Do you limit your criticism, avoiding going on and on?

SCORING: Add up your numbers. The closer you are to 10 the more constructive your criticism is likely to be.

Receiving Feedback

Team members also must learn to *receive* feedback well. They need to listen first without evaluating and then try to understand the feedback from the perspective of the person giving it. Team members who are open to good constructive criticism can help find alternative ways of doing things, and help develop the best ways of working together in the future.

Feedback Loops

A team might consider creating a feedback loop, which is any mechanism that enables the team to discuss issues as needed. A feedback loop might take the form of peer evaluations or regular team meetings. Feedback loops help team members stay involved in communicating with each other.

Evaluations

Regular team evaluations are an important aspect of maintaining an effective team. A team leader is responsible for facilitating the group's constant and consistent improvement. Team members need to evaluate themselves, individual team members, and the team leader. They need to do overall evaluations of how the team functions, evaluate the progress of team goals and the commitment to the team mission. They should ask, for example:

- Are the team norms and values still in place?
- Does the mission need refining?
- Is the team fulfilling its mission?

The team and the team leader should also review recent outcomes and determine why they were successful or why they were not.

External Feedback

Just as we individually learn about ourselves by learning how others perceive us, a team learns a great deal from external feedback. It is vitally important for a leader to seek feedback from superiors, from members of other teams in the same organization, from customers/clients, and from professional organizations that specialize in team building. External feedback is similar to listening for self-awareness. The more we hear about ourselves, the better we understand the image we project. We are offered valuable insight into who we are, which gives us information to analyze how we might change and improve.

Sometimes, external feedback tips us off to problems we do not see ourselves. For example, one management team at a large nonprofit was convinced it was doing well. Certain external factors also indicated the team was doing well. Their division did very well in terms of production and marketing of their services. Yet a senior manager in another division of the organization informed the team leader she felt the team was headed for trouble because of subtle problems she sensed between Asians and others on the team. At first the team leader didn't accept her judgment, but he kept a close eye on team relations. At a team meeting a short while later, certain anti-Asian biases among some team members became apparent. The team went though a diversity team-building course a short time later.

This example also stresses the importance of team leaders actively seeking feedback from team members. The team leader in the example above did not properly seek feedback from the Asian team members. If he had, he might have been able to deal with certain attitudes before they became problems.

Feedback for the Team Leader

A good team leader must also constantly seek feedback on her own job. Leaders can only keep their teams moving toward their missions if they are aware of what they are doing well, and what they need to do to improve.

Receiving leadership feedback is not always a given. It must be actively sought; from team members who work with the leaders every day and whose trust they need to lead the team, as well as from outside the team. Leaders should seek feedback for their own performance as well as the team's performance. Remember that self-awareness is a goal for every leader.

Gaining Respect and Trust through Feedback

Leaders also gain the respect and trust of their team members when they seek feedback. When a superior makes people feel that their opinions are valued and that they are respected, they work better, harder, and offer more of themselves. They feel a part of the process. The more people feel their opinions are valued and respected, the more they are willing to state their opinions, and the better their criticisms become. The whole team benefits from good constructive criticism .

It is vital that, as a leader, you do everything necessary to help your team continuously evaluate you. You must work on your self-awareness to be sure you know how well you are facilitating the evaluations. You also need to model giving feedback and model being a good team member in general. As a communicator and a leader, you need to respond to your team members empathically, and metacommunicate.

Metacommunication and Teams

Metacommunication is another important aspect of continuous evaluation. As noted in Chapter Five, metacommunication means communication about communication. On a diverse team with many possible communication styles, it is easy to miscommunicate. So talk about the communication. Make sure you are creating shared meanings. Discover what is good about how you are communicating, and discover how the way you are communicating could improve.

Team-Building Exercises

A part of continuous evaluation is continuous team building. By doing team-building exercises on a consistent basis, you make sure the team is growing together and maintaining its effectiveness. Team-building exercises also give you a way to evaluate how the team is doing. By gauging how the team-building exercise works, you can tell if the team is coming together or coming apart, and what should be done to keep the team functioning together, including whether more or fewer team-building exercises are needed. We look at two team-building exercises below.

"**Machines**." The exercise I call "Machines" is fun and helps a team explore how its members communicate and work together. Break the team into groups of four to seven people. In a hat (or other container) have slips of paper with the names of machines that use moving parts written on them. You might have one that reads "washing machine," for instance, another that reads "typewriter," and another that reads "copy machine." (Or each group can determine its own machine.)

The groups then go off to private areas, where they determine how they will communicate, without using words, what their machine is to the other groups.

When the groups come back together, each group gets in front of the others and does a little performance. Usually there is a lot of laughter, and an amazingly fast determination of each machine.

The debriefing concentrates on what they learned about communication, how they worked together to determine how to communicate their machines, and how it felt to perform as a group in front of the others to communicate their machines.

Team-Building Meeting. A leader can use the following exercise as a simple team-building exercise. During a team meeting, ask a few open-ended questions that help the team examine and best utilize its diversity. Questions could include:

- What does our team do best?
- How does our diversity help us?
- What problems does our diversity create?
- What other problems does our team have?
- How could we improve?

The Team-Building Circle

By doing these team evaluations, we have come full circle. We are once again acknowledging our diversity, once again celebrating our humanity, building on our uniqueness, establishing our mission, and developing a supportive climate. The team-building process should never stop. Team-building is an ongoing requirement for success in a diverse workplace.

Diversity Tips

1. Embrace differences—find and value the differences of team members.

2. Celebrate humanity—understand that no matter how different we are from one another, we have more commonalities than differences.

3. Build on uniqueness—build on the strengths and styles of each team member.

4. Establish the team's mission—help a team focus by writing a mission statement that includes the team's values, norms, and goals.

5. Develop a supportive climate—model being supportive, facilitate support, and encourage team members to support each other.

6. Continuously evaluate—the team needs constant evaluation to keep improving.

7

Managing Conflict

*Communicating effectively with those with whom
we have fundamental disagreements is more
difficult but often more important than
communicating with those we like.*

Roger Fisher and Scott Brown[1]

Juanita is a manager at a large government
agency in the Southwest. Every day she eats
lunch in the lunchroom with friends who are
all native Spanish speakers, and they generally
speak Spanish. The lunchroom is, in fact, mostly
segregated. There is some intermixing, but
mostly the whites, African Americans, and
Latinos sit in separate groups.

Juanita is confronted in her office one day
by Laura, a white colleague. Laura is angry that
Juanita and her friends always speak Spanish

in the lunchroom. She wonders if they are criticizing the company, the other workers, or America. She wants them to speak English.

Laura is also upset by the general segregation in the lunchroom. She feels the company needs to do something to bring people together. Juanita tells her that lunchtime is the one time of the day workers can get away from the rules of the workplace and relax, but Laura insists that segregation is bad for the employees' relationships, as they work in teams on their jobs.

The two women begin to argue. Laura's accusations offend Juanita, especially her insinuations concerning loyalty to other workers. Grant, an African American mid-level executive, hears the confrontation and steps in to mediate. Laura asks Grant what he thinks about the segregation in the lunchroom, but he tells her he plans to keep out of the argument and simply help the two of them resolve their differences.

Juanita asks Laura if she is paranoid about people of color taking her job. Grant points out that Juanita is attacking Laura instead of discussing the issues. He asks them if they see any options. He has them explore their concerns. Laura repeats her concerns about segregation in the lunchroom affecting teamwork on the job. Juanita expresses her concern that there needs to be time and a place where employees can get away from the job and relax. Grant asks them to analyze those concerns, and they realize they are both concerned about employees working together and doing a good job.

In the end, the two women agree that they cannot stop other employees from doing what they choose in the lunchroom, so the scope of the conflict is beyond them. They both finally hear each other's side, though. Juanita responds to Laura's concerns by offering to speak English when Laura is present. Laura thanks her, and says she understands better why the Latinas speak Spanish, and she will not rush to judgments. She also apologizes to Juanita for accusing her, and other employees, of disloyalty to the organization.

Grant showed excellent leadership skills by mediating a type of conflict often present in diverse organizations.

Conflict is inevitable. Wherever there is more than one person, more than one idea, or more than one way of doing things, there will be disagreements. The potential for conflict in a diverse organization is even greater than in a homogeneous one. We cannot prevent all conflict, nor should we try to. Conflict fuels organizations. It increases innovation, production, and energy in the workforce. Yet conflict can also tear an organization apart, creating dysfunctional work teams, drop-offs in production, and distrust throughout the organization. Executives must understand the benefits conflict offers organizations, as well as the harm it can do. And they must learn how to prevent conflict that is destructive, resolve conflict to facilitate people working together, and manage conflict for the benefit of the entire organization.

THE BENEFITS OF CONFLICT

Webster's Unabridged Dictionary defines conflict as "incompatibility or interference, as of one idea, desire, event, activity, with another; discord of action; antagonistic state of action, as of divergent ideas, interests, or persons; hostile encounter."[2] While this definition includes words with negative connotations for organizations, such as "antagonistic" and "hostile," much of this definition points to why conflict is vital for keeping organizations thriving.

Without conflict, workers may become complacent. Any organization without incompatibility of ideas does not have enough ideas circulating to keep it honest and moving toward the future. Organizations need to be internally challenged to keep on top of their missions, and to stay competitive.

Conflict Generates Ideas

Dynamic organizations often encourage some types of conflict in order to find the best ideas and the best solutions to their problems. One training organization uses the approach that people need self-esteem to be good managers, but that having many managers with high self-esteem leads to conflict. Their trainers first work on building participants' self-esteem, then do exercises to generate ideas. Conflict arises when people with high self-esteem throw many varying ideas on the table. The higher the self-esteem, the more ideas are thrown out, creating more conflict. People tend to become invested in their ideas. The trainers then teach participants how to resolve these conflicts so that the company remains innovative while people learn to work together.

Organizations that use this type of approach can derive the benefits of conflict. Many innovative organizations encourage new ideas, and allow open disagreement, including disagreement with the ideas of the CEO. They have learned to work together to resolve disagreement in ways that allow the best ideas to be determined and used.

The Benefits and Risks of Expressing Emotion

In many cultures, shows of emotion are not acceptable. In American culture, however, expressing emotion is not only considered healthy, it can be beneficial to the organization. Expressing emotions can lead to creative problem-solving by making relevant issues discussable and enabling people to clarify misperceptions. Showing emotions also connects people more personally, joining us in real relationships.

Keeping feelings pent up leads to people staying closed, not communicating their problems, becoming frustrated with the job, encourages mistrust, and sets the stage for the eruption of emotions in a nonproductive way. It is at times good for executives to express feelings such as "I feel frustrated," or "I feel stepped on," or "I don't feel heard." By expressing your feelings, others will more likely express theirs.

Use care in expressing emotions, however. Expressing emotions can help create an open environment in the workplace, but it can also be destructive and can harm an executive's image. The executive might be seen as weak, unreliable, or even unfit for the job. Emotions need to be expressed with control. Express emotions with an understanding of the reasons for expressing them and respect for the harm they can do.

THE NEGATIVE SIDE OF CONFLICT

While conflict can be a beneficial force in organizations, much conflict is unwanted, unproductive, and destructive. Many employees, including managers, do not work well when there is conflict. Some cultures in particular do better without conflict, as do people with certain family backgrounds or psychological makeups. There is some evidence that suggests that witnessing conflict can lower production of work groups.

Petty arguments serve little purpose in organizations and hurt the interpersonal relationships of employees. Conflict around things that cannot be changed is also never beneficial. People can gripe all they want to about a certain company policy, for instance, but if that policy is mandated by federal law, there is nothing the organization can do about it.

Many conflicts related to diversity conflicts are never beneficial. Racism, sexism, ageism, homophobia, and intolerance of people with disabilities lead to conflict. Organizations must have zero tolerance for all of these "isms." Hatred and intolerance only lead to unresolvable arguments and the inability of people to work together.

Sexual harassment is a particular kind of discrimination that causes serious production problems, including illness, turnover, and lowered self-confidence. A *Working Woman* survey in 1988 indicated that many women lose self-confidence and experience production drop-offs just knowing sexual harassment exists in the organization.[3] Victims of sexual harassment experience a 10 percent drop in production, according to that survey, and those who witness sexual harassment experience a 2 percent drop-off.

More recent studies indicate similar results. With the high turnover (an estimated 15 percent of women change jobs due to sexual harassment), work teams need to regroup and learn how to work together all over. The conflict generated by sexual harassment harms organizations in financial ways as well. The most recent estimate is that a successful sexual harassment suit will cost an average-sized company $8.7 million.[4]

Even when people don't think they are hateful, intolerant, or discriminatory, their actions can lead to destructive conflict. Gays and lesbians, older workers, and people with disabilities often talk about the ridicule they face and the pain of being the subject of demeaning jokes. Conflict often erupts in these situations. When an aggrieved party lets it pass, it is often at the expense of his or her self-esteem. People who have lowered self-esteem, who feel dis-included, work less productively.

Preventing Nonproductive Conflict

In organizations with people from diverse backgrounds, the possibilities for misunderstandings are great. Conflict can occur merely because one person misunderstands what another person has said or how they have behaved. The principles of effective communication outlined in Chapter Five are helpful.

Executives who are good communicators are less likely to get involved in nonproductive and petty conflicts than others and are in a position to prevent conflict among others. As Dean Barnlund explained:

Good communicators assume that others are well-intentioned. This assumption is based on the recognition that, at any given moment, each of us does the best we can according to our experience, knowledge, attitudes, and skills.

Good communicators treat communication as two-way interaction between two or more participants who are equally responsible for the creation of meaning and the outcomes of the communication.[5]

Listening to Prevent Conflict

Executives who are good communicators keep an ear to the workplace. Using all of the interpersonal skills in an executive's tool kit is vital to determine if hateful activities and other harmful conflicts are occurring. Listening, especially, is something an executive needs to do to be sure to detect any nuance of these negative behaviors. It is also vitally important to be aware of the types of conflict that might cause harmful problems.

Skills to Reduce Misunderstandings

No matter how well we communicate, though, misunderstandings do happen, especially when the communication is between or among people from different backgrounds. It is vital to be as constructive as possible in our communication when such misunderstandings occur. Following are five constructive response skills that can be used to reduce and respond to misunderstandings.

Support. Show that you recognize and appreciate the efforts people make to communicate well and work together. For example, if a person who generally is helpful in reducing discriminatory or noninclusive behavior makes a statement that troubles you, say: "Sam, I notice that you are encouraging the quieter members of our team to express themselves more—thank you for that." Then ask a question to help him reconsider what he said. Communicate empathy, tell the person you understand he is uncomfortable in a certain situation, and then ask him to help you be sure you understand him correctly. By showing support first, you create an environment that helps the other person reconsider the communication without feeling put on the spot.

Clarify. Paraphrase. Ask for more information to increase your understanding of someone else's perspective. For example, perhaps a woman has suggested something you disagree with. Ask her to clarify the communication and expand on it so you are sure you understand her correctly. "Kumiko, you mentioned that you don't think men should receive the same kind of parental leave benefits that women have—can you tell me more about that?" Be descriptive. When you say, "I notice that . . ." you raise awareness without blame.

Suggest. If you hear something clearly stated but think it is not a good idea or a correct reason, suggest something different. You might self-disclose your feelings: "I feel . . .," "I believe . . .," "I am offended . . ." Or you could open your suggestion/response with: "Perhaps we could try . . ." or "how about . . ." Be specific, but be creative. For example, if someone states that your project didn't go well because the people involved can't work well together, you might suggest: "Perhaps we could change our usual seating arrangement so we'll have an opportunity to interact with different people." Use humor where possible.

Request. We often need to establish boundaries when a communication situation gets out of hand. Ask for cooperative action to solve a problem to encourage a sense of shared responsibility. For example, "How can we talk about this account without getting too emotional and misunderstanding each other?" You might need to specifically say that certain remarks have a certain effect and request they not be used. Another way to use requests is to directly encourage others to share the responsibility for change. For example, "Maria, you've done excellent work on this kind of account before. What are your thoughts?"

Insist. More serious instances of inappropriate behavior require a quick response. For example, "Eric, that's the third time you've interrupted Celeste during this meeting. Please let her finish what she's saying." Or, "Gwen, I've asked you before. Please do not tell jokes about older people in this office."

Use "I" Statements

Often we know there is no misunderstanding. Someone has said something or behaved in such a way as to upset us. It is important not to inflame conflict where it might be nonbeneficial. In such cases, the use of "I" statements can help prevent further conflict and still make the point clearly.

If you begin statements about your perceptions, thoughts, feelings, or preferences with the word "I," your statements will have a more positive impact on others. Using "I" statements can also clarify your own perceptions, thoughts, feelings, or preferences.

Compare "I feel that you _____," with "You _____." Starting with "I" makes it clear that you speak from your own point of view and that others may not have the same perception. Beginning with "You" is more likely to convey the impression that you blame the other person and that you are certain only your perceptions are correct. If the other person then responds with a "you" statement, assigning responsibility back to you, negative feelings may escalate and it may become harder to reach an understanding.

Below is a template for "I" statements.

"I have a concern. When I saw your **behavior**, **consequences** happened, and I felt **feeling**. I'd like **positive outcome**. How would you feel about trying **preference/ suggestion**?

When you create your own "I" statement, alter the template as needed to fit the situation. By making an "I" statement, you tell the person you value the relationship and take responsibility and ownership for your feelings and perceptions.

The following is an example of an effective "I" statement:

I need to talk with you about a concern. Today at the meeting I suggested a new accounting procedure. You didn't acknowledge it, or me. A few minutes later Mike made the same suggestion, and you praised him. I felt angry and undervalued, and didn't want to contribute anything else to the meeting. I'd like you to make more of an effort to recognize what I say.

It is important to practice using "I" statements as much as possible. Following is an exercise for creating "I" statements in which you:

- Identify a shared problem, claiming ownership of your perception of the problem;

- Describe the behavior that presents the problem;

- Express the concrete consequences of the problem;

- Express the feelings you experience as a result of the problem; and

- Express a preference for change, asking for ideas and perhaps offering suggestions.

"I" Statement Exercise

For the following situations, develop "I" statements that convey your concerns. Follow the order expressed in the section above. Imagine you want a coworker or supervisor to:

1. Stop telling gay-bashing, sexist, racist, ageist, or other jokes.

2. Address you in the way you would like to be addressed.

3. Speak less frequently in meetings to allow more participation for quieter people.

4. Stop touching you in a way that you find inappropriate and uncomfortable.

5. Stop leaving out members of a particular group when planning projects or activities.

Think of other specific situations or relationships about which you have concerns. Construct an effective "I" statement to inform the person of your concern, and to help look for ways to improve the situation.

Avoid Conflict-Increasing Behaviors

While constructive responses and the use of "I" statements can help prevent or reduce conflict, it is important to avoid certain behaviors that have the potential to increase conflict. It is also important to know what these behaviors are in order to recognize them when they are being used by others. Remember, though, that some cultures value conflict, while others disapprove of conflict. Try to understand the background of the person as well as their behavior.

Avoid Appeasing. Often people say "I don't care" when they feel the opposite, or they go out of their way to tell a person everything is OK when it is not. If problems are not acknowledged, they don't get fixed. Don't appease a person at the expense of resolving the misunderstanding or disturbing behavior. If you are communicating with a person who is appeasing, try to understand the person's background. Some cultures tend to be much more appeasing than others. It is important to draw out an appeasing person (possibly with Proactive Listening) to be sure you understand whether or not a problem exists, and what that problem may be.

Avoid Suppressing. The fires of conflict can be fueled by name-calling bouts, interrogations, or unsolicited advice, sermons, and unwanted diagnoses. These things are used to dominate and control, and fail to reduce the conflict. All of these behaviors prevent others from being able to clear any misunderstandings or otherwise help the situation. If we are communicating with a person from a nondominant culture, these behaviors reinforce our dominance, and make the other person more anxious about attempting any future communication.

Avoid Blaming. Conflict can create hostility and anger. It is easy to blame others for our feelings when we feel upset. When we put the blame on others, though, it adds to the already destructive environment. Conflict can be the result of one person doing something wrong, or one group behaving a certain way. More likely, however, conflict is more complex. We sometimes blame conflict on our differences instead of really looking at the problems. Blaming others never accomplishes anything except granting momentary feelings of self-satisfaction. The problems still exist. Accept responsibility, not for the cause of the conflict (unless you realize you are the cause), but as an equal in the communication situation.

Avoid Distracting. By switching modes, or changing the subject, we prevent discussing the things that need to be discussed in order to clarify misunderstandings and prevent the conflict from happening again. We tend to distract when we do not know what to say, feel panicky, or want to avoid any conflict.

Avoid Controlling. There are many ways to control communication. True communication, however, means sharing the creation of meaning. By controlling the communication we fail at communication, and use our power unfairly. It is important to give the other person a chance to save face, to say he or she is sorry, to make sure we understand each other.

Nonproductive Interpersonal Conflict Strategies

Joseph DeVito notes that any conflict is easier to create than prevent and resolve. His list of unproductive interpersonal conflict strategies emphasizes the types of things we do when we argue with another person.[6] By avoiding these things, we will help prevent and reduce conflict.

- Avoidance: May be physical, emotional, mental or intellectual; avoidance tactics include changing the subject, abstracting the problem, and refusing to negotiate.

- Minimization: Making light of conflict, either with humor or by minimizing the consequences.

- Blame: Avoiding responsibility (and subsequent problem-solving) by putting all the blame on someone or something else.

- Silencers: Crying, yelling, or other extreme emotional outburst which prevents any communication from taking place.

- Gunny sacking: Storing up grievances, as in a "gunny sack," then expressing them one after another when arguing about another matter; prevents discussing the matter at hand while opening old wounds.

- Belt Lining: Hitting below the belt, or "pushing buttons," especially when you know someone is sensitive about the subject, or with conflict in general.

- Manipulation: Diverting conflict by acting in a way to get the other person into a noncombative frame of mind.

- Personal Rejection: Withholding affection or respect, and getting the other person to break down to regain what's withheld.

- Force: Use of physical force indicates a total breakdown in communication.

RESOLVING CONFLICT

Whatever communication skills we possess to help prevent and avoid conflict, conflict still will occur. An executive needs to understand conflict and get as much benefit as possible from it while helping people work together. It is vital for executives to know how to resolve conflicts they are involved in and how to resolve conflicts they witness or that are brought to their attention.

The first step in conflict resolution is understanding the communication styles people use during conflict situations. Some conflict styles are shown in Exhibit 7.1.[7]

Understanding Conflict Styles

One way of understanding conflict styles is to look at them in terms of the animal metaphors noted in Exhibit 7.1.[8] One drawback to these metaphors, though, is that they are culturally specific. These animals do not have the same connotations in all cultures. Groups may wish to substitute metaphors specific to their cultures. The process of finding those metaphors increases the understanding of the conflict styles.

The Teddy Bear (Smoothing). Relationships are of great importance to teddy bears, while their own goals are of little importance. They think that conflict should be avoided in favor of harmony. Discussing conflicts hurts relationships, teddy bears feel, or hurts the people in the relationships. Teddy bears give up their individual goals to preserve the relationship. They try to smooth over conflict out of fear of harming the relationship.

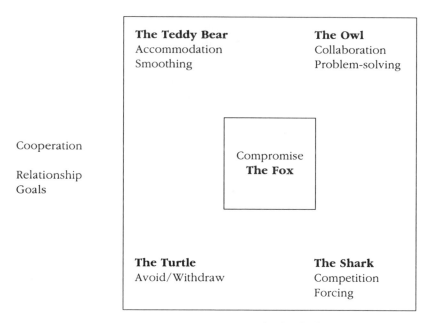

EXHIBIT 7.1
CONFLICT STYLE CHART[7]

Source: Adapted from Thomas Ruble and Kenneth Thomas, "Support for a Two-Dimensional Model of Conflict Behavior," *Organizational Behavior and Human Performance* 16 (1976): 145; and unpublished work of Karen Lovaas.

The Turtle (Withdrawing). Turtles withdraw into their shells to avoid conflicts. They give up on both personal and relationship goals. They stay away from the people they are in conflict with, and if they can't do that, they stay away from the issues in conflict. Turtles believe it is hopeless to try to resolve conflicts. They feel helpless. They believe it is better (or easier) to withdraw physically and mentally from conflict than to face it.

The Fox (Compromising). Foxes are moderately concerned with both the relationship and their personal goals. Foxes seek compromise; they are willing to give up a part of their goals if they can persuade the other person in the conflict to give up part of theirs. They seek a solution to the conflict in which both sides gain something and both sides lose something. They seek the middle ground between two positions. They are willing to sacrifice a part of their goals and relationships in order to find agreement for the common good.

The Shark (Forcing). Sharks try to overpower their opponents by forcing them to accept their solution to the conflict. The relationship doesn't matter to sharks as long as their personal goals are reached. No cost is too high. They don't care for the needs of others. They don't care about being liked or accepted. Conflicts are win/lose situations. Sharks want to be the winner, to gain a sense of pride and achievement. Losing means weakness, inadequacy, and failure. They try to win by attacking, overpowering, and intimidating others.

The Owl (Problem Solving). Owls highly value both their own goals and their relationships. Conflict to them is a problem that needs a solution. They do everything they can to find a solution that satisfies both their goals and the other person's goals. Owls see conflict as a means of improving relationships by reducing tension between those involved. They attempt to begin a discussion that identifies the conflict as a problem. Owls maintain relationships by seeking solutions that satisfy both themselves and others. They are not satisfied until those solutions are found and the negative feelings and tensions between the people in conflict have been fully resolved.

Alternative Views of Conflict

We often view conflict resolution strategies in win/lose terms. After all, we might think, one side must win a conflict, which means one side must lose. Or is that what conflict means? The Shark looks at conflict strictly in win/lose terms and will do everything possible to win. The Turtle and the Teddy Bear don't seem to care about winning or losing. Both want to avoid conflict. This avoidance behavior creates lose/lose outcomes. One side might appear to be the winner, but in truth the conflict is never resolved, so both sides lose in the long run. The Fox and the Owl, though, seem to offer a chance for an outcome where both sides are satisfied, where there are no winners or losers. Let's look at both a little closer.

The Fox compromises, which seems to be a good choice in that there is cooperation and each side wins a little. The problem is that each side also loses a little. In fact, both sides might lose so much that no one really wins. Compromise as a word has many positive connotations. We might refer to a politician or business executive as a good compromiser, meaning she gets the job done by being flexible enough to give up a little in order to get something back.

But compromise also has negative connotations. Would you want to be in a compromising situation? Would you want your integrity compromised? In the long run, compromise should be avoided because it probably creates an outcome where there are no winners or losers, only sides that have given up too much.

The Owl stresses collaboration. The problem-solving approach to resolving conflict is generally accepted as a win/win. When we problem-solve, we do all we can to assure that both sides get as much as possible, rather than looking at the situation as a win/lose proposition. In other words, when we are collaborative, one side doesn't have to lose for the other side to win.

Integrative and Distributive Strategies

There are many similarities between strategies for resolving conflict and strategies for negotiations. Current negotiation theory looks at two types of strategies: *distributive* and *integrative*. Distributive negotiators look at a negotiation as a pie that needs to be sliced. Each side gets a piece of the pie. Integrative negotiators look at the pie and try to find a way to make it bigger. While the distributive negotiators attempt to win the negotiation, the integrative negotiator looks for a win/win outcome, where the best solutions for everyone involved are attained.

Consider an organization about to endure a strike by its technical employees. The distributive approach would be to find a way to win as many points as possible. (Either side can be distributive. If it is management, then they want to maintain or lower current costs, among other things. If it is labor, they want to get more pay and better benefits.) The integrative approach would look at what is best for the organization, which includes what is best for *both* management and labor.

Problem-Solving as a Win/Win Strategy

Of all the conflict styles noted above, only the problem-solving approach is integrative. The problem-solving conflict strategy, like the integrative negotiating strategy, seeks a win/win outcome. It does not look at the pie (in this case the conflict) as a fixed entity. It looks at the process and the effects of the outcome on all involved parties. The other four conflict styles all require one side giving up something, as if there were no other way, as if the pie was a fixed size.

When we *compromise,* both sides make sacrifices in order to resolve the conflict. Compromise tends to be an expedient method for resolving the conflict as soon as possible without looking at ways to truly satisfy all parties. Forcing and accommodating both view conflict in terms of one side giving up in order for the other side to win. The avoiding style wants no part of conflict, so does nothing to resolve it. Avoiding is distributive in that the pie is fixed, and untouched.

Using the Problem-Solving Collaborative Approach

The problem-solving collaborative approach to conflict resolution is the method leaders must learn in order to create benefits out of conflict. The following adaptation of Michael Doyle and David

Straus's approach to problem-solving meetings offers a good example of how a problem-solving approach to conflict resolution can work. In this example, assume that a small group is doing the problem-solving, and that a facilitator is helping the process. The approach can work with almost any number, so long as multiple parties are trying to find solutions to a problem; they are attempting to resolve conflict.

Doyle and Straus's six step problem-solving model[9] contains the following steps:

1. Define

2. List/vent

3. Brainstorm

4. Evaluate

5. Develop action plan

6. Implement

Step 1. Define the Situation

Develop a definition of the problem that is concise (at most three sentences) and flexible. A good working definition can be vital to the success of the problem-solving session. It can help create feasible, creative solutions. A bad definition can assure failure of the session.

Don't limit possibilities by definition. If your organization has Christian fundamentalists and gays who have severe difficulties working together, don't define the problem: "The Christians and the gays will not work together." If phrased that way, the only solution would be to find ways in which the two groups don't have to work together. The logistics of the organization, among other things, probably prevent that possibility.

Create a nonspecific, non-binding definition. In the above scenario, a good definition might be: "We have to find ways to get all groups in the organization to be productive." That definition opens the doors to many possible creative solutions.

Think about using a "gap statement" as a definition, which says: "We're here now; we want to be there tomorrow." Again in the earlier scenario, a good working definition might be: "We have one group that strenuously prefers not to work with another group. We need to find a way to get all groups working and satisfied."

Step 2. List What's Wrong with the Current Situation

Do not think of solutions during this step. This is the time to explore what members of the meeting see as the problems associated with the situation and their impact. It is not the time to think of solutions. Be sure the facilitator tells anyone who offers solutions to please wait till step 3..

Vent! The facilitator should try to get everybody in the session to express their feelings. Venting helps put people into a psychological state of readiness for problem-solving.

Try to see the full scope of the problem. In creating a full list of what is wrong, the group will understand more clearly how large, or small, the problem is. This information might also change the way the group feels about the situation, leading to a need to return to Step 1 to redefine the situation. For example, the situation might be clarified in such a way that group members see a better definition. Or the problem might be shown to be too large for the meeting to tackle, leading to a definition that allows the group to try to fix only a part of the situation. (If the group goes back to Step 1, there is no need to return to Step 2. After the new definition is determined, the group should move on to Step 3.)

Step 3. Brainstorm Solutions

Use the following brainstorming guidelines:

1. Hold off on judgment.
2. Let the creative juices flow. Think of as many ideas as possible.
3. Piggyback ideas—let new ideas expand on earlier ones.

4. No idea, no matter how stupid sounding or unfeasible, is to be rejected.

5. Record all ideas.

6. Think about using turn-taking to get it started, but don't stick to it too long. Allow for a free flow of ideas.

Brainstorming works because it increases involvement and participation, produces a large number of ideas in a short time, and encourages creative thinking. There should be absolutely no evaluations of any ideas during this step! The facilitator needs to stop any comments about the feasibility of any idea.

Step 4. Evaluate

First, organize the ideas generated in Step 3. Combine and collapse categories where overlap occurs.

Cross out unfeasible solutions. There probably will be a good number of unfeasible, even ridiculous, suggestions. Delete them as quickly as possible.

Finally prioritize the ideas. Try to put order to your list by evaluating how good the remaining solutions are. You might need to develop a criteria list (how soon solutions can be implemented, costs, social concerns, and so on, or list the pros and cons of each possible solution). You also might need to vote on the top three choices. The goal is to decide on the top few solutions that are most workable.

Step 5. Develop an Action Plan

Now it is time to plan the who, what and when of actions to be taken. Group members need to commit to doing specific things by specific dates. If your plan includes names of non-group members, you need to specify when and how to get these people involved.

For instance, in the previous example, your plan might include the need for a certain concession by the supervisor of a specific shift. You need an action step, then, that states: "Jane (a group member) will meet with the supervisor on September 21 to gain his commitment."

Step 6. Implement

The final step is follow-up and evaluation. This step takes place after the session, though plans for a future meeting to evaluate the action plan should be made during the initial problem-solving session.

FINDING THE BEST SOLUTIONS

There are other models for problem-solving. Perhaps the most common is one that simply defines the conflict, examines possible solutions, tests and evaluates the solutions, then rejects the proposed solutions and seeks new ones or accepts the proposed solutions and resolves the conflict. Successful organizations don't mind some conflict as long as it leads to the best solutions. A problem-solving strategy helps you find those solutions.

Using Other Conflict Styles

There are times to use other conflict communication styles. Effective leaders use a variety of styles, especially in a diverse workplace where the differences in styles of the people in the organization mandate a diversity of styles in handling conflict. Some cultures respond to conflict differently than others. There are also issue, relationship, and time factors involved.

- Use the accommodating strategy when the working relationship is of utmost importance.
- Use compromise when issues are complex and fairly important, solutions are difficult, and you have enough time to effect a compromise that is fair to all parties.

- Use forcing when the issue is very important to you, when you know you are correct, and when there is little time.

- Use the avoiding strategy when there is time pressure and the issue is not so important.

- Use the collaborative approach as often as possible.

- Of course, time plays an important role in your use of problem-solving strategies; you need enough time to find the best solutions and test them.

Mediation

The ability to mediate effectively is a very important leadership skill. Mediators must remain neutral at all times, and manage the process of the resolution. Help the parties in conflict talk with each other and acknowledge a conflict exists. Steer them toward a problem-solving strategy, and facilitate the session. Maintain fairness by keeping the session focused on the issues and not the personalities. Do everything you can to keep the parties searching for solutions, rather than establishing responsibility for the conflict. Examine why each party has taken the position it has, and help them discover the reasons behind their positions. While discovering their reasons, they might find common ground. Help them build their relationship from that common ground. And finally, be sure that all parties understand, accept, and commit to the solutions they arrive at.

Atlas Headgear, Inc., based in Phoenix, uses a worker self-mediation technique that has produced very positive results. Ninety-four percent of the organization's employees are Asian and Latino. Many of them are immigrants, and 80 percent are women. When conflicts between groups arise, the company's bilingual employees mediate the conflicts, bridging the gap between employees who speak English and those who do not.[10]

Ten Pitfalls to Avoid as a Mediator

Below is a list of pitfalls mediators can fall into.[11] Avoid them whenever possible.

1. After you have listened to the argument for a short time, do not begin to nonverbally communicate your discomfort with the discussion (e.g., sit back, begin to fidget).

2. Do not communicate your disagreement with one of the parties through facial expressions, posture, chair positions or reinforcing comments.

3. Do not say that you shouldn't be talking about this kind of thing at work or where others can hear you.

4. Do not discourage the expression of emotion by suggesting that the discussion would better be held later after both parties have cooled off.

5. Do not suggest that both parties are wrong, pointing out the problems with both points of view.

6. Do not suggest part-way through the discussion that possibly you aren't the person who should be helping solve this problem.

7. Do not try to get both parties to attack you.

8. Do not minimize the seriousness of the problem.

9. Do not change the subject (for example, do not ask for advice to help you solve another problem).

10. Do not express displeasure that the two parties are experiencing conflict (e.g., do not imply that it might undermine the solidarity of the work group).

MANAGING CONFLICT

Conflict will occur, and in specific instances should be encouraged. Managers often pay lip service to the importance of conflict but do everything they can to avoid it. Such avoidance supports Warren Bennis' statement: "American organizations . . . are underled and overmanaged."[12] It appears easier to avoid a sticky situation than to confront it. A leader, however, doesn't look for easy ways out.

An effective executive will seize on conflict as an opportunity to enhance the organization. He or she will know how to recognize conflict, have the ability to determine how beneficial and how destructive it is, understand the styles of those in conflict, and be able to facilitate problem-solving to get the most benefit out of the conflict.

Managing Diversity Conflict

Conflict caused by style differences based on culture, gender, age, or physical abilities can also be healthy, as long as executives and managers manage it well. Effective executives use conflict to motivate those in conflict to learn what their differences are and use them to create a better working relationship. The parties need to step back, look at what happened, and learn to live with and utilize their differences.

Imagine that two people from two different backgrounds come into conflict because each has a different idea of how a job needs to be done. An executive who understands managing conflict will help the two people solve the problem. By integrating what they know, they might be able to find a better way of doing the job than either of their individual methods. That is the essence of problem-solving, and the essence of managing conflict.

Managing the Worst Diversity Conflict

An effective executive, a leader, looks at conflict as an opportunity. Organizations must have a policy of zero tolerance for racial hatred, discrimination, sexual harassment and other forms of sexism, and homophobia. Yet a good leader can derive some benefit from even that type of conflict.

For instance, if a Saudi Arabian man is having trouble with a white lesbian, there exists the potential conflict based on cultural differences, gender, and homosexuality. This provides a good opportunity to talk about all of those issues. The dialogue can begin to get the issues into the open and dealt with. Once they are dealt with, an organization can get on with its work.

It is possible that such a dialogue will create energy and an increased ability to work together. As the parties begin to understand each other, their productivity will increase. It is also possible that such a dialogue will develop more creative thought, which can be transferred to the job and may increase innovation. When managed well, conflict can lead to new ideas and help people work together.

Diversity Tips

1. Conflict can be beneficial to organizations.

2. Some types of conflict are harmful.

3. Constructive response skills aid in resolving conflict productively.

4. "I" statements tend to reduce conflict.

5. Avoid conflict-increasing behaviors and unproductive interpersonal conflict strategies.

6. Use problem-solving to best resolve conflict.

7. Mediate conflict between others to facilitate their working together.

8. Manage conflict for the benefit of the entire organization.

CHAPTER

8

The Words of Leadership

You can't just put something on an overhead transparency slide that says "vision" and expect to inspire people, unless you really mean it, believe in it, live it.

James C. Collins and Jerry Porras[1]

Antolitec Industries was near bankruptcy, looking for a possible merger. The board of directors looked at its options and decided to replace its CEO with Collette, a dynamic executive who had been promoted to Senior Vice President for Marketing only six months previously. She'd risen fast in Antolitec and had built relationships with people at all levels of the organization. She also had a national reputation as an Olympic Gold Medal-winning swimmer.

As CEO, Collette immediately launched a campaign of weekly motivational addresses to the entire company through a special radio hook-up, telling employees how the organization was changing and why she needed and valued their help. Her almost-daily walking tours of the corporate offices created a palpable air of enthusiasm.

Collette also embarked on a national speaking tour and appeared on television talk shows to get out the word about Antolitec's new vision, a vision "shared by everyone in the organization." The business obituaries were premature, she said. Like her own come-from-behind victory in the Olympics, Antolitec had turned the corner and was going to make a comeback.

In three years, Antolitec has totally turned around. Its sales are up, its financial picture is superb. Production is back above the industry standard, and there is practically no turnover. As Antolitec begins to grow back to its pre-downsizing size, it is attracting the top people in its field.

It is difficult to tell how much Collette's speaking ability helped in Antolitec's revival. There is little doubt, however, that her communication skills helped turn the company around. She motivated her employees, inspired them to share her vision, and convinced the outside world that Antolitec was coming back strong. Motivational speaking is probably the best known of leadership traits. Political, religious, nonprofit, and business leaders all use words and rhetoric to motivate people to share their visions, to inspire and persuade them to accept each other, and to tolerate each other's differences and cooperate with one another.

WORDS, REALITY, AND CULTURE

We use language to create and understand meaning. No matter what we hear, see, or experience, we give it meaning by putting words to it in our heads. Nonverbal communication might mean "no words," but it communicates meaning to others because of the words *others* use to understand it. Meaning is in symbols, in words.

Our words create our reality—they shape our understanding of everything we know. We are socialized by our words. One person's "chair" might be totally different from another person's "chair." We create realities by stating, and thinking, the words that form in our minds. Ideas and abstractions, such as love and democracy, exist because we say they exist. Even physical "realities" such as color exist within a cultural context. (Cultures without words for colors are "culturally colorblind"; they see no colors.) In essence, words give meaning to our existence.

Words, likewise, give meaning to culture. One of the main functions of language is to communicate ourselves, our uniqueness. A culture living within another culture creates its own language, such as a dialect. A dialect is a subculture's way of taking ownership of the language of the dominant culture, to separate itself. A culture needs to identify, define, and communicate its own special qualities, values, and sense of self.

Language and Diversity

Language by its very nature is ambiguous. Words are symbols, and often have more than one meaning. When people are from different backgrounds or have different frames of reference, the same words or actions may have different meanings to them than they have to you. What you think you see or hear is not necessarily what you are seeing or hearing.

Like nondominant cultures, each organization within a culture develops its own language that expresses its core values and identity. The language may include acronyms, specific words used to mean things other than the usual uses of the words, ways of dress, and behavior. The corporate culture of Apple, for instance, is quite different from the culture of IBM. Apple even used that difference as part of a major advertising campaign.

Leaders and Organizational Culture

Leaders understand their organizational cultures, and know how to communicate within them. They help shape the culture with their use of language. They can share their visions with words and create the realities of those visions because of their mastery of words.

Mary Kay Ash created Mary Kay Cosmetics with a vision of helping women earn equal money to men.[2] She created an organizational culture that emphasized many of the values discussed in Chapter Four in the section on gender style differences. Women have been socialized to see the world in terms of support and networking. Ash set up her company with weekly unit meetings in which women share their experiences, support each others' difficulties, and applaud each other's successes. As founder, she consistently speaks to values concerning equality. The organizational culture reflects, is defined by, the language of its founder.

RHETORIC AND COOPERATION

We humans are each separate and distinct, yet we cooperate in intricate waysto create culture. Kenneth Burke defined rhetoric as the use of language to induce cooperation.[3] In other words, rhetoric is the function of language that creates cooperation among humans. It is the function of language that enables us to form cultures.

The implications of this definition of rhetoric are vital to the study of leadership in organizations. An executive's primary job is to get people to cooperate, to work together to get the job done, to accomplish a mission, vision, or goal. Even in competition between organizations, there is cooperation; without two or more parties agreeing to compete, usually under agreed guide-lines, there is no competition. Executives use rhetoric constantly.

Rhetoric and Leadership

Many people misunderstand rhetoric as political speech, yet the concept applies to two-person communication, small group communication, and written communication as well as to public speaking. No matter what other terms we might use to describe how we create cooperation among people, they all are still rhetoric. Leaders must learn to use rhetoric effectively.

Robert Haas of Levi Strauss understands the power of rheto-ric. His speeches around the country motivate American business in general, but help Levi Strauss in particular. His speeches inspire a wide diversity of people to want to work for his company, and as a result many of the best minds in the clothing industry come to Levi Strauss.

Persuasion and Cooperation

Leaders learn that rhetoric means not just what you say, or how you say it, but how you reach your audience, how you identify your real concerns with theirs, and how you truly move them. Much of what we are talking about concerns the word *persuasion* because cooperation implies persuasion. We *persuade* people to cooperate, to share our meaning, to share our visions.

David Pottruck, President and CEO of Charles Schwab and Company, is a man whose persuasive abilities create cooperation. He has been a motivating force behind his company's drive for a diverse workforce in an industry known for its white male dominance.[4] His speeches and other communications to the employees of Schwab have created an environment of coopera-tion around a very difficult topic. It is the kind of cooperation necessary to keep the organization a leader in its field. Schwab will not be surprised by Workforce 2000 because the company's organizational values, communicated by Pottruck and other senior executives, already embrace the reality of the diversity that is here today and will be greater tomorrow.

Symbolic Action and Rhetoric

Leaders like Pottruck persuade with more than their words. Their actions are consistent with what they say. Their convictions are strong and are communicated in everything they do. Leaders often model behavior or lead by *doing* more than by *saying*. What any of us does communicates what we believe. Humans ascribe meaning to what we see including other people's actions. As a result, all human action is symbolic action and is in the realm of rhetoric.[5] The following addition to the case that opened this chapter illustrates how symbolic action is rhetorical.

One of Collette's early decisions as CEO of Antolitec was to do a cultural audit to determine who was employed by Antolitec and how they reflected the company's customer base. The results spurred her to recruit, in spite of the recent downsizing, from a variety of underrepresented groups, especially in the marketing and research and design departments. She made it a point to welcome each new recruit and to communicate her pleasure that the organization was moving into the future.

As Antolitec began the move to more diversity, Collette's weekly in-house radio speeches often emphasized the importance of a diverse workforce. She created a weekly column in the company newsletter focusing on differences among people. She also initiated company-wide diversity training with an emphasis on communication and made it a point to get news coverage of her participation in a training session with non-management personnel.

Collette helped her company's turnaround by communicating her conviction. There was no doubt of her commitment to a diverse workforce. Her participation in the non-management personnel training session communicated both her belief in the training and her identification with all employees. As a result of her words and actions, employees at Antolitec shared her vision. They worked together, cooperated, to create the reality of that vision.

Rhetoric as Magic

The concept of creating reality sounds magical, and indeed it is. Rhetoric can be viewed as magic (and magic can be viewed as rhetoric).[6] Ancient taboos kept people from deviating too far from cultural norms. They created reality with words. If people did something too deviant, chances were that something bad would happen to them. The magic was that the people were so persuaded by the cultural norms that things happened. To this day, we refer to masters of rhetoric, to the best speakers and writers, as "spellbinders."

Leaders and the Power of Language

Rhetoric does not have to be magical, it only needs to be understood. Leaders who understand language, its beauty, its power, communicate their visions and motivate and inspire people all around them. They understand the best way to use language is not with sound bites, or with empty statements with little meaning. They know they cannot prove their virtuosity with style over substance, or prove their intelligence with boring facts and statistics. They know that the true beauty and power of language is that it can be used to help people see possibilities.

Anita Roddick, Managing Director of The Body Shop International, is one such leader. She consistently uses language to help people see the possibilities of what business can be. Her vision is one in which business takes an active role in doing good in this world, in which business is an agent for social change. She speaks often, she speaks passionately, and she speaks her values. Roddick uses rhetoric to inspire not only those who work for her, but others in the business community and society as a whole as well.

RHETORIC FOR SELF-AWARENESS

Diversity and leadership skills begin with self-awareness. Understanding rhetoric helps people understand *what* persuades them, *why* it persuades them, and *how* they can be less susceptible to

persuasion. People who don't understand how they are persuaded, or even *if* they are being persuaded, make better fol-
lowers than leaders.

Persuasive Tools

Understanding the meaning and importance of rhetoric is only
a first step. It is vital for leaders to know specific persuasive tools
that help create cooperation in a diverse environment.

The basic tool of rhetoric is identification. An identification
is a connection a communicator makes with his or her audience.
A communicator needs to identify with the audience on different
levels. In other words, he or she needs to show the audience
they are connected in specific ways. In particular, you persuade
people, you induce cooperation, by communicating yourself,
expressing emotion, and using logic and argumentation.

Communicating Yourself. You communicate yourself by using
your own unique voice, your experiences, your values, your
knowledge, and identifying your interests with those of your
audience.

Expressing Emotion. Identify your real feelings with the feelings
of the audience by expressing emotion.

Using Logic and Argumentation. Identify your information, your
evidence, with your audience's sense of logic and connection to
the information.

THE MEANING OF COMMUNICATING YOURSELF

One of the main things any of us communicates is our self. This
is one of the functions of language. On a macro level, we
communicate our culture. On a micro level, we communicate our
self. Everything we say says something about who we are. Good
salespeople can sell almost anything because they know how to
sell themselves.

Who we are creates identifications with our audience that will
determine whether or not they will believe us. Generally, our

"voice" tells an audience who we are. Our voice is our style, how we phrase things, the words we use, our syntax, the way we speak or write. Our voice gives our audience insight into our character, credibility, sincerity, honesty, and leadership. Leaders find their voice, and use it to identify with their audiences.

Communicating Authenticity

Terry Pearce, in his book *Leading Out Loud,* writes that America is practically crying out for leaders we can believe in.[7] He talks about authenticity and conviction. Leaders need to speak in a way that wins the hearts and minds of their audience, he says. Much of a person's conviction is intangible; an audience senses it by the way the speaker communicates. Leaders need to learn who they are, what their values are, and be able to communicate themselves as real, as authentic.

Tarah Walters shows how authenticity can be communicated throughout an organization and beyond. Walters is President and CEO of University Hospitals Health System, University Hospitals of Cleveland and one of the few female chief executives of a major healthcare system in the U.S. While she speaks about diversity often and outlines and explains her own organization's diversity strategy, she stresses in particular the economic benefits that an intelligent, well-thought-out diversity strategy can bring to an organization. Walters emphasizes that it is vital for top leaders to communicate in every way they can how and why diversity is important to organizational welfare and prosperity. Her commitment drives individuals throughout her organization to share her vision.[8]

Identifying with an Audience

Leaders need to communicate in ways that identify themselves with their audience. Identifying yourself with your audience, like the CEO who talks to her employees like she was one of the boys (I use this metaphor intentionally), makes its members feel you are like them. It persuades them to listen and believe you because it helps them believe you share their interest and believe in their values.

Ross Perot is a billionaire businessman turned politician, yet he sounds like a common person. We don't expect that particular communication style from someone with so much power and money. We expect a loftier style of speech. He identifies with the common person because he sounds like one. Jimmy Carter's wearing jeans in his inaugural parade symbolically identified him with the common person. So did Franklin Delano Roosevelt's fireside chats.

Identification and Words

We need to identify with our audience in more explicit ways as well. We need to *tell* its members that we are like them. If we are speaking to a group of people we know eat at fast-food restaurants, we might drop in a line about a meal we ate at McDonald's the other day. A simple line like that can connect us to our audience, showing them that we are no different from them.

Telling Stories to Communicate Who You Are and Enhance Your Credibility

Terry Pearce often tells the story of helping his oldest son move to San Diego to start college.[9] When it was time to leave, Terry felt a sense of loss, and a sense of accomplishment. He tells this story in part because it helps him connect to his own convictions about delegation and letting go. He also tells it because he knows that everyone in his audience is somebody's child, and many have children of their own. He knows he will identify with his audience.

The best speakers are good storytellers. Ann Richards, former Governor of Texas, is known for her sometimes humorous, sometimes poignant, always dynamic storytelling. Ronald Reagan was known as "The Great Communicator" in large part because of his ability to tell stories. Yet stories work in writing as well as in speaking. Barbara Kingsolver, Stephen King, and Anne Rice all write great stories. Examples written as stories can enhance a proposal as well as a speech.

Stories are one of the best, if not *the* best, rhetorical tools. They connect you with your audience and with your message, and connect your audience with you and your message. Telling stories can enhance your credibility. As a speaker or writer, you need to show your connection to your topic and set yourself up as an expert, or as a person who has studied the topic. Stories help show your audience how you identify with the topic.

Identify Yourself with Your Topic

You can establish your credentials in many ways, both formal and informal. Give your audience the reasons why you are presenting your message. Show why you know what you are talking about.

If I was talking to a group of people about diversity, for instance, I would establish my credentials as a person who has studied intercultural communication, rhetoric, and other areas of communication, teach managing diversity and communication skills to MBA students at a major university, and consult in the areas of diversity, leadership, and communication, including creating training programs for employees at all levels in diversity, gender communication, and sexual harassment. I also might tell them that I am a Jewish man who has lived in non-Jewish communities all of my life, that as a child I lived in a Moslem country for three years, that as an adult I have lived and worked in Christian, Buddhist, Hindu, Moslem, Shinto, and animist countries and communities, that in the early seventies my wife and I both worked half-time as we co-parented. I know what it is like to be a part of the nondominant culture, to feel alone, underappreciated, discriminated against, and misunderstood. When I speak and tell my audience about these aspects of my background, I do so to establish that I am a credible expert.

THE POWER OF EXPRESSING EMOTION

Expressing emotions in a rhetorical context means communicating emotions in such a way that your audience feels what you feel, or what you want its members to feel. Your audience identifies with your feelings, which motivates them to take action. It is a powerful persuasive tool. You are appealing to the hearts of your audience. When we honestly express how we feel, our audience feels it as well. We are communicating our emotional selves, and the emotion itself persuades our audience.

Storytelling and Emotional Identification

Sometimes you can use emotion to help your audience identify with the people you speak about. Perhaps the best way to persuade with emotion is to tell good stories. Stories can make people laugh, cry, or march out of a room in anger. When stories are told in such a way that the audience identifies with them, you elicit real feelings from your audience. You get your audience to identify so strongly with the feelings that you create cooperation, you persuade them to work with you or work together for a common goal.

For example, perhaps a coworker is trying to persuade you to work against an initiative that would make it against the rules for Filipinos to speak Tagalog to each other on break. She tells you a story about how she once worked in a foreign country, and even though she spoke the language of that country, she spoke English with other English speakers as often as she could. She could feel more relaxed when she spoke English. She didn't have to put effort into every sentence. If this coworker had identified with you on other levels so that you believed and respected her, then you would likely sympathize with her position and better understand the Filipinos.

Your coworker might make the story even more emotional by telling you how one day while she was working in that country several coworkers severely criticized her for her rudeness in speaking English, and how she cried and couldn't work any longer that day. You might feel real disgust with the people who made her cry, and in turn feel disgust with the people who would be so insensitive to the Filipinos.

Kenneth Burke said that the best identifications occur when the voice of the speaker or writer reflects our voice within. In the example above, you would readily identify with the Filipinos if you had worked in a foreign country yourself and had experienced the same type of rebuff as the woman who told you the story.

Women who come forth with sexual harassment stories about public figures elicit a lot of anger from many women. They believe these stories because the tellers identify with them so strongly. They have experienced similar situations or felt similar feelings themselves. These stories motivate many women to oppose the public figure who has been accused.

Analogies and Metaphors

Another way to use emotion to persuade your audience is through analogies and metaphors. They can be short, or told as a story. Analogies and metaphors engage us, make communication more interesting. We also have to process them, which helps us understand their meaning in a fuller way.

Analogies create a connection to something else the audience identifies with. For instance, I might say that creating an environment uncomfortable for a diverse workforce would be like opening a hotel with uncomfortable beds; anyone with any sense would stay away. With this analogy I identify with my audience's feelings about comfort, and also with all the emotions that surround the idea of attracting quality people to the organization.

Metaphors are the ultimate symbols. A metaphor represents one reality as a different reality, which suggests a likeness between the two. For example, Jesse Jackson calls his political organization the Rainbow Coalition. The rainbow metaphor gives us an image of beauty and harmony, denoting the beauty of diversity. A rainbow is made up of many different colors, each distinct yet working together to make a beautiful whole. A rainbow denotes prosperity (the gold at the end of the rainbow), calm in the face of trouble (even though it is raining, the warmth of the sun shines through), and peace (all the different colors coexisting and enhancing each others' existence).

THE IMPORTANCE OF LOGIC AND ARGUMENTATION

Your personal identification with your audience and its emotions motivate your audience, but without logic, there is no long-term persuasion. I might convince my audience that I know what I am talking about, and am sincere. I might get them so angry at a personnel analyst, for instance, that they'll get up and start to march to his office, only to stop halfway there to ask themselves why they are so sure the analyst is to blame for anything. You need to give your audience good, sound reasons to prove to them that you are right.

Barry Eckhouse, in his book, *Competitive Communication,* says that modern business is an argumentative practice.[10] He means that business is based on competition. One business competes with another for customers. One manager competes with another to get her idea adopted by the organization. This competitiveness stimulates growth and ideas, among other things. Competition implies opposing views, differing ideas or agendas. Whoever can state the best idea, or argue the best case, wins the competition.

If I want to convince you that diverse teams are more creative than homogeneous teams, for example, I had better give you better arguments than the person in the next office who has statistics proving that homogenous teams work so well together that they develop more ideas in the long run. My arguments need to be based in logic, not emotion, because your decision may affect the long-term effectiveness of the organization. My arguments need to provable and viable.

An argument is a statement that makes a claim. This claim needs to be backed with sound reasoning. When you argue, you need evidence that what you argue is correct. Logic and argumentation are complex subjects that are not within the scope of this book. I can say, though, that logic and argumentation really boil down to identification.

Argument is only as good as the connection it makes with your audience. Your logic needs to identify with the audience's sense of logic.

Logic and Culture

That sense of logic relates to your audience's culture. Logic, like rhetoric, is a function of language. Our grammar, the way we organize our language, gives us a sense of order and creates what we understand as logic. As a result, logic is culturally based. Languages are quite different from one another, so the logic of one culture does not always fit with the logic of another culture.

What might seem logical to native English speakers might seem illogical to the Japanese, for instance. English-speaking logic is based on a linear grammar. We ask "why" and expect a "because." In Japanese, the grammar is more complex, more circular, or what I call "spiral." The Japanese expect a lot of "going around" a topic before coming to any conclusions. Some Americans think that the Japanese way of doing business is not always "logical," and they are right, from a limited cultural perspective. When we look at cross-cultural persuasion, we need to be extremely aware that what we "know" to be a logical argument may not work. Your audience needs to identify with the logic, and can only do that if the argument identifies with the audience's culture.

The audience needs to identify with evidence as well. I can give you all the evidence in the world that a diverse marketing team knows how to sell to a diverse customer base. Yet if you do not identify with the evidence, my argument will go nowhere. The evidence might be our organization's improved sales during the fourth quarter, but you might believe that the fourth quarter is always good for our organization, that our new hot salesperson made a big difference, and that other companies also showed a gain that quarter. I must either connect you with the evidence I use or with the reasons I present.

Logic and Storytelling

One primary way of making a logical connection is through storytelling. Aristotle wrote of logic as consisting of two types of reasoning, deductive and inductive. Deductive reasoning is the use of the syllogism. It means drawing conclusions from premises. In other words, from certain information, you can draw a valid conclusion. The conclusion is correct as long as the information is correct. Aristotle said that inductive reasoning, on the other hand, means proof by example. When you use stories as examples you are using inductive reasoning. These stories must be representative of what you are trying to prove. The problem with inductive reasoning is that a good counter example can successfully refute what you have attempted to prove. Examples must be representative of a common experience in order to be successful arguments. For the example of the Director of Human Resources who didn't support on-site day care, many stories could counter her argument that because she was able to breastfeed and keep on working, other women can, too. For one thing, she was speaking about a different era, an era in which fewer women in the workforce were breastfeeding mothers. Any number of stories can be found about women of her era who were unable to work because they breast fed, or who quit breastfeeding in order to keep working.

A good example can prove many things, though. A good story is concrete. People tend to believe real experience. People connect with stories. They are the most powerful form of persuasion you can use.

Inoculation

As powerful as your stories and logic may be, your persuasion may fail if you do not inoculate your audience. Inoculation means dealing with arguments contrary to your point of view. In medicine, an inoculation is a preventative procedure to help a person resist a certain disease. The person is "inoculated," or given a small amount of the disease (or something very similar to the disease). The person reacts to the inoculation by building antibodies that help him or her resist the disease. Without inoculation, the disease may overcome the person.

In persuasive speaking, to inoculate our audience against contrary ideas we need to think of arguments against our po-sition, present them, and either present counter-arguments or show why they are not very important. We need to be careful only to present counter-arguments that we are sure our audience might think of. Otherwise, we give people reasons to be against our position that they may not have thought of themselves.

In speech, you might inoculate early, to deal with resistance, and later, to deal with major arguments against your position. Be sure you have swayed people before offering reasons that are in opposition to your point of view. In writing, your inoculations should be late in your piece and should be full arguments. Because they are on paper, readers will have a chance to thoroughly think about them.

Remember that the best audience identification occurs when the voice of the speaker or writer reflects the audience's voice within. Inoculation means trying to hear the voice of your audience, and assure that you have addressed all of its concerns. If you do not inoculate, contrary arguments, like an uncontrolled disease, may eventually destroy any persuasion you might have accomplished.

Diversity Tips

1. Words and language have great power as well as beauty.

2. The culture of your audience, both in terms of where its members come from and the culture of your organization, determines the most effective ways of communication.

3. Rhetoric can create shared vision and inspire people to cooperate.

4. To communicate yourself, use your own unique voice, your experiences, your values, and your knowledge, and identify your interests with those of your audience.

5. To express your emotions persuasively, identify your real feelings with the feelings of the audience.

6. Logic and argumentation are crucial to persuasion. Information and evidence must identify with the audience's sense of logic and connection to the information.

7. To inoculate your audience against contrary views, deal with arguments that members of the audience know which contradict your point of view.

8. Remember the importance and power of storytelling.

9

Leading Change

*If you see in any given situation only what
everybody else can see, you can be said to be so
much a representative of your culture that you
are a victim of it*

S. I. Hayakawa[1]

Textec, a moderate-sized textile firm with a
diverse customer base, decided to interview Jenny for a marketing position. She im-
pressed the committee with both her academic
and professional backgrounds. Her recommen-
dations were exemplary.

The interview was comprised of two days
of talking with people at all levels of the
organization. She sailed through the first day.
Almost everyone who talked with her, including the search committee, the director of

marketing, and several other executives, rated her extremely highly. All recommended that she be hired. The second day was a series of meetings with various designers, production workers, and support staff.

Jenny went into that second day wearing a confident manner that was soon shaken by the first interview with the head of plant maintenance. He was a Latino who spoke English with a thick accent, and Jenny seemed to have a hard time understanding him. She also seemed extremely uncomfortable during her meeting with a designer, a woman from Sri Lanka who kept circling Jenny's seat in her motorized wheelchair. Jenny ate lunch with a team of production workers and twice rolled her eyes at their eating manners.

As a result of the second-day interviews, Textec did not offer Jenny the job.

Jenny's story is a little different from the other cases that open the chapters of this book because it is a story told at Textec all the time. Managers tell it to new employees, to each other, to employees at various levels of the organization, and even to people outside of the company, including customers. The story underlines some basic values of Textec's corporate culture. Jenny was not flexible enough to work with people whose differences she did not understand. She was arrogant to those she felt were of lower stature. Her communication skills were not good enough, not only for the corporate culture, but because the company didn't think she could market to its customer base.

Stories like Jenny's are used often in organizations. Storytelling is one way to inform employees of an organization's core values, objectives, vision, and mission. Another important tool is the company's mission statement. Both of these means of communication help people understand the organization's culture. They can also be used to help an organization change.

Benefiting from Change

Today's organizations are in a state of flux. There are many reasons for the changes, but one of the most important reasons is diversity. As organizations become more and more diverse, there is more need to find new ways of doing business. Organizations can benefit from making the necessary changes to adapt to new environments, and today's leaders can implement the changes through the use of good communication skills.

The globalization of business, competition with organizations from other countries, new technologies, and environmental concerns are a few reasons for the difficult changes today's organizations are going through. But it is diversity, as both a cause and effect of all these forces, that stands out as perhaps the most problematic reason. Only the problems of diversity reflect all of the problems embedded in society, such as racism, sexism, homophobia, and ageism.

The question is: How do we create a workplace where the potential strengths of diversity will overcome the problems and benefit the organization? How can we assure everyone in the organization that diversity will be the benefit we claim it will be? The challenge is for leaders to help create a workplace that embraces diversity to yield the benefits only diversity can bring.

Legal Compliance

In the past, it was possible for an organization to thrive while allowing one culture to dominate it, subjecting all nondominant cultures to nonessential roles. Those days are over, for legal reasons if not for plain business sense. There are laws against discrimination, Affirmative Action laws to create fair hiring practices, the Americans with Disabilities Act to protect people with disabilities, and other laws to protect the diverse elements of the workforce. (That diversity makes good business sense still appears to be of little meaning to some organizations.)

The laws have led to too many organizations that merely comply (often grudgingly) with the laws. They "accentuate the negative" rather than attempting to get the most out of the diversity they now have. They do little training, little education

They change few structures and attempt to maintain the same organizational culture. They shoot themselves in their organizational feet because the changes are not being managed, just accepted as fait accompli. These organizations do nothing positive to utilize their diverse workforce.

Redefining Organizations

Forward-thinking organizations are redefining their organizations by getting input from all new employees, as well as from long-time employees. They are attempting to understand what changes need to take place, and how best to go forward with them. Changes include reengineering their organizational structures and modifying their core values. These organizations are committed to ending all forms of discrimination, for good business reasons. The changes they bring forth assure that everyone in the organization works together, and these organizations grow and prosper.

LEADING AND CHANGE

It takes leaders to effect these changes. Leading change means finding ways to get people involved in the process of change. It means communicating the changes in a way that helps people understand them and become inspired to embrace them.

Two of the critical tools in leading this kind of change are mission statements and storytelling. By creating mission statements that reflect the new values and encourage the respect of all members of the workforce, an organization makes an issue of diversity, and communicates to its employees, to its customers and clients, and to society at large that it values that diversity. Finding the emerging stories, and telling them in such a way that they reinforce the values surrounding diversity, helps organizations change smoothly and with the commitment of the employees. Stories define, refine, and reinforce the nature of the organizational culture; they tell what the organization is about.

Leading change means understanding and promoting the organization's vision. James C. Collins and Jerry I. Porras, in *Built to Last: Successful Habits of Visionary Companies,* offer examples of visionary companies. One thing Collins and Porras note is that what is needed is a core ideology that exists . . . not merely as words but as a vital shaping force."[2]

Creating Change with Creative Tension

Peter Senge talks about creative tension as a way to create and lead change.[3] He says that the enlightened leader will create tension by clarifying vision (saying where he or she wants to be) and telling current reality (saying the truth about where his or her organization is). He says that the tension can be resolved either by raising the current reality toward the vision, or lowering the vision to the current reality. Obviously, we want to move toward our vision, and good leaders learn to use that tension to create their realities.

As Senge notes, leading change with creative tension is different from leading with problem-solving. With problem-solving, existing problems motivate the change. The problems, or current reality, create the need for change. With the concept of creative tension, the leader's vision provides the motivation for change. Change comes from what the leader wants to create.

Senge notes that the idea of creative tension is not new, that leaders have talked about it in the past. He quotes Martin Luther King: "Just as Socrates felt that it was necessary to create a tension in the mind so that individuals could rise from the bondage of myths and half truths . . . so must we . . . create the kind of tension in society that will help men rise from the dark depths of prejudice and racism."[4]

And so must America's organizational leaders. They must raise the current reality of their organization to their vision of embracing diversity. They can start by creating mission statements.

MISSION STATEMENTS

Mission statements have been around for a long time, and in the past have often been merely marketing slogans or statements designed to make stockholders feel good about the company they held stock in. The purpose of mission statements is changing, though. They are now used for internal as well as external purposes. Mission statements let employees know what the purpose, goals, and values of their organization are. They unify employees, and give them a sense of purpose. Michael Applebee, vice president of organizational development for Charles Schwab, calls his company's statement ". . . the heart and bone marrow of our organization."[5] A mission statement defines the organization's mission, telling its employees, customers, stockholders, and society what it stands for and where it hopes to go.

The "New" Mission Statement

Mission statements often go beyond the normal scope of business. Progressive companies, ones with vision, see beyond the immediate bottom line, and realize that the community's good (be that community local, global, or customer-based) is the good of the organization. Some organizations even believe in doing something for ethical and spiritual reasons, irrespective of normal good business practice. Mission statements often express those lofty goals for the same reason as the purpose story discussed later in this chapter. They give the employees, stockholders, and customers a chance to think in larger terms than the organization, to feel they are doing something for the greater good.

As organizations change, they need new mission statements. The new statements reflect the new values, new goals, new vision. They help define the "new" organization.

A Leadership Tool

Leaders use mission statements to get everyone in their organizations to buy into the values, goals, and vision of the organization. Leaders who want to build a foundation for the future, leave their mark on their organization, and promote change use mission statements as a way to bring people together and move the organization forward. They have become a tool for change.

Mission Statements for Embracing Diversity

A number of organizations use diversity as a cornerstone of their mission statements. Levi Strauss & Co. includes a section subtitled "Diversity" in its "Statement of Company Mission and Aspirations." The "Aspirations for the Company" section begins with two introductory paragraphs, which end: "In order to make our aspirations a reality, we need: . . ." What follows are sections on New Behaviors, Diversity, Recognition, Ethical Management Practices, Communication, and Empowerment. The Diversity section reads:

> **Diversity:** Leadership that values a diverse workforce (age, sex, ethnic group, etc.) at all levels of the organization, diversity in experience, and a diversity of perspectives. We are committed to taking full advantage of the rich backgrounds and abilities of all our people and to promote a greater diversity in positions of influence. Differing points of view will be sought; diversity will be valued and honesty rewarded, not suppressed.[6]

Many people feel Levi Strauss attracts some of the best workers in the garment industry because of its diversity and related personnel policies. It is known as a great place to work. The company's use of diversity in its mission statement exemplifies the values of the organization.

Other companies also use mission statements to exemplify company values and move people toward embracing diversity. Mission statements like this one from United Airlines help members of the organization understand how diversity can be a benefit to the organization.

United Airlines Mission Statement

The people of United are dedicated to being the world's best airline.

Ever pursuing a passion for innovation, we will never be satisfied with the performance of today.

We strive to serve you with style and sophistication, building upon our unparalleled legacy of professionalism and technical leadership.

>Uniting a broad mosaic of cultures and traditions,
>we hope to foster economic prosperity and inspire
>human understanding.

The United Airlines' statement does not use the word "diversity," but the implication is clear. Jeffrey Abrahams, in his book *The Mission Statement Book,* studied 301 corporate mission statements and found the word "diversity" only 26 times.[7] Organization leaders need to take better advantage of their mission statements' ability to gain commitment from everyone in the organization on diversity issues.

Who Creates the Mission Statement?

Mission statements often are now being written by teams of managers, or teams of a cross-section of employees. This process of creating mission statements ensures that everyone in the organization not only understands the company's mission, but by having helped to craft it, believes in it as well.

Having many people write such a statement can be a complex process, but it can be well worth the effort. Yet as Terry Pearce said, after helping guide Charles Schwab through such a process, "There's a tremendous power with 75,000 people pulling together. The main result is not a statement on the wall but an alignment of people."[8]

Bringing Diverse Elements Together

Diversity needs an alignment of people. The workplace needs an alignment of people. The process of writing a mission statement, of bringing together the diverse elements of an organization and getting them to work together to craft a statement that reinforces the very thing they are doing, can be a powerful tool for creating an effective diverse workplace.

A leader needs to balance empowering the writers with the job of writing the statement, while assuring that the shared vision of the organization is communicated. The writers need to know that the statement should make as much connection with diversity (among other things) as possible. The statement should use the word "diversity." It also needs to use inclusive language. It is also up to leaders to frame their organizations' missions so they inspire change and help people embrace the diversity of their organizations.

Framing the Mission

How an organization's mission is framed can determine how successful it is in reinforcing and changing the organization's values. *Framing* means shaping the message to communicate what we want it to say. We might frame our mission in simple terms that flatly state who we are and where we want to go. Or we might frame our mission in a way that inspires us. The best mission statements are inspirational; they help motivate the reader to strive to accomplish the mission.

Jay Conger relates the story of two stonemasons who were helping to build a church.[9] When asked what they were doing, one said he was cutting stone, while the other said he was building a great cathedral. The second mason used language in a more far-reaching and meaningful way. Leadership means to embody that ability to use language, to articulate an organization's mission and communicate it in ways that inspire.

Steven Jobs, known for his unique style of leadership, framed his vision of NEXT, the company he started after he left Apple, as revolutionizing the educational system of the nation. Conger, among others, points out that he could have merely said he wanted to build computers and sell a certain number of them to a particular market.[10] Instead, he inspired his employees with his vision, giving them a sense of excitement about their organizational goals.

THE MISSION WRITING PROCESS

The process of writing the mission statement needs to be developed in such a way that the statement communicates what is necessary to inspire change.

The Committee

The following method creates a high-level committee that looks into such areas as target audience, format, language, an overview of the ideas that need to be included, and logistical matters such as meeting times and places. They also select who will write the statement.

The writers of the statement should be a good cross-section of the organization. Even if you determine you want only managers, they should reflect the diversity of the organization. It is better to include non-management personnel, though. You will assure a more committed workforce if you do.

The First Meeting

The next step is an adaptation of a four-step Advocating Quality program I developed with Rick Isaacson of San Francisco State University. Try to get a group of twelve employees. Divide them into three groups of four, Groups A, B, and C.

All twelve employees attend the first meeting together, and discuss the organization's mission. It is a good idea to have the organization's leader (CEO, Executive Director, President) either write a vision statement for the group to read or attend the first part of the meeting and discuss his or her vision and sense of the organization's mission. The group needs to explore its own ideas of what the organization's mission is as well. The members need to discuss their thoughts on the goals of the organization, its purpose, and its core values. They especially need to discuss diversity. They might look at the following questions.

- How important is diversity in the organization?
- How can our diversity positively affect the organization's mission?
- How do individual values lead to different notions of what being a part of an organization means?
- How do differences in values shape employees' acceptance of and compliance with organizational values?

- How do diverse values come together to form the organization's values?
- What effect does the diversity of the organization have on the organization's customer/client base?
- What effect does the diversity of the organization's customer/client base have on the organization?

The group also needs to discuss what should be in a mission statement, and what form their statement should take. They might want to look at a variety of existing mission statements.

The Second Meeting

Before the second meeting, each person needs to write his or her own statement. The statement could be the entire mission statement, if you are planning a short one, or a plank of a mission statement. Perhaps it is the vision statement, or the values statement. All twelve people should write the same plank.

At the second meeting, the committee members split into their three groups. People from group A give their unsigned statements to the people of Group B, Group B passes to Group C, and Group C gives theirs to Group A. Each person in a group takes one anonymous statement, and by turns, reads it aloud to the other people in his or her group.

The group members who are listening should be in Active Listening mode. They should not attempt to interpret, evaluate, or let their feelings affect what they are listening to while the statement is being read. When each reading is complete, the group members should paraphrase what they've heard until they agree that they understand what the writer wrote. They then discuss each statement critically, evaluating what was written.

The discussions will be open. No one has a vested interest in any of the statements, and no one knows of the personal involvement they might have with the author of the statement. People are free to look at the ideas and the writing, without worrying about personalities. The discussions will generate many new ideas.

The groups each get an assignment to rewrite their statement, this time with the benefit of having heard the statements others wrote and having been involved in the discussion about them.

The Third Meeting

At the third meeting, each group member reads his or her own revised statement in their small group. The group then shapes a statement as a group.

The Fourth Meeting

At the fourth meeting, all twelve people congregate to hear the three final products. They might choose one, or they might further shape a final product.

After the Meetings

An organization might decide to have the same twelve people meet several times for each plank, or, if the organization is large enough, have different groups of twelve work on different planks. If the mission statement is to be short, only one group is needed. It often is best for a final small committee of six to eight people to look at the final product, clean up any inconsistencies in tone, repetitions, or any other details, and present a finished mission statement. This might be the initial committee that selected the writers and determined the logistical and other matters.

The top people in the organization need to give final consent. Mission statements do require top-level approval. They need to reflect the shared vision of the organization.

The statement also needs to be distributed to everyone in the organization, with an explanation of the process used to write it. One idea is a large "coming out" party. Assemble as many people in the organization as possible and introduce them to the statement. Acknowledge the people who wrote it. Frame the event in such a way that everyone there feels they have been a part of the process. The more people feel they were a part of developing and finalizing the statement, the more they will be committed to it.

STORYTELLING

Once an organization has a new mission statement, it needs to continue communication in support of the statement's message. Storytelling is one of the most powerful tools a leader can use to promote change, reinforce values, and back up the organization's mission.

Storytelling is as old as human culture. Before humans could write, they passed on their cultures, histories, values, and ways of living to future generations with stories. Even after people had invented writing, many cultures continued to tell stories to create the realities of their cultures, to maintain their ways of being. Many cultures remain storytelling cultures today.

The Bible is a collection of stories originally told from one generation to the next. Hindu mythologies are based on stories, as are the mythologies of the Apache, Bantu, and Shan. These stories tell these cultures who they are, structure their societies, and create their realities.

Storytelling as Rhetoric

In Chapter Eight, we discussed the notion that language is culture, that words create reality, that rhetoric is the function of language that induces cooperation and creates cultures. Storytelling is a form of rhetoric, perhaps the oldest form. Stories and myths do more than reinforce a culture's core values; they help create the culture. They give meaning to people by giving them their identities.

For a number of years, much has been written about organizational myths and metaphors. Told as stories, or just hinted at in a variety of subtle ways, the mythologies define and fine tune the organizational cultures in which they occur. Stories create the common identifications of the culture.

For example, an organization that is a leader in sales and repairs of copy machines began when its founder started a small business repairing copy machines out of the back of his truck. To this day, that story is repeated, and the company retains an entrepreneurial and customer-driven culture.

This story is one of many. Just about every organization has a few stories that people refer to when discussing why their organization is the way it is, what their purpose is, and what their values are. Jobs and Wozniak started Apple in their garage. Wells Fargo Bank still uses the stagecoach as a constant reminder of its long-term commitment to serving its customers no matter what predicaments they may face.

Storytelling and Leadership

Storytelling is a leadership skill. Political leaders have often been good storytellers. Abe Lincoln was. Ross Perot and Jesse Jackson are. Business leaders also tell good stories. Mary Kay Ash and Lee Iaccoca tell great stories.

David Armstrong, in his book *Managing by Storying Around: A New Method of Leadership*,[11] offers insight into the ability to tell a story in such a way that it helps shape the organization. Armstrong believes that storytelling should be an integral part of the organizational culture. He uses storytelling in place of policy and training manuals. In his book, Armstrong details twelve reasons leaders should tell stories in organizations.[12]

1. *Storytelling is simple.* We've all told stories since childhood. People with all levels of education both tell them and listen to them.

2. *Storytelling is timeless.* Storytelling is ageless, fad-proof. Once you start using storytelling as a leadership tool you can keep doing it, without needing to learn every new fad that comes along.

3. *Storytelling is demographic-proof.* No matter how your workforce changes, everybody, regardless of age, race, or gender, likes to listen to stories.

4. *Storytelling is an excellent way to pass along corporate traditions.* Stories show what a company believes in, and tell people how to behave. Through stories, you learn what an organization is like.

5. *Storytelling is the best form of training.* Armstrong uses stories to tell people how his organization does things, including letting people know what will get them promoted or fired. He

developed a storybook that is filled with all the stories he has created and told in his organization.

6. *Storytelling is a way to empower people.* Stories set guidelines. Once the story is fully understood and internalized, the employee works on his or her own.

7. *Storytelling is a wonderful form of recognition.* When leaders tell stories about their organizations, they often use real examples. When they name names, the people named are recognized as being an integral part of the organization.

8. *Storytelling is a great way to spread the word.* Stories are told to everyone in the organization, so the things an organization believes in are constantly reinforced.

9. *Storytelling is fun.* Stories are an enjoyable way to learn about things.

10. *Storytelling is a great recruiting and hiring tool.* Armstrong uses his storybook as a way to show new recruits what the company is about. He also uses stories as ways of determining who he wants to hire. He will tell a story, and see how a potential employee reacts.

11. *Storytelling is a great sales tool.* He uses his storybook again. Customers learn what kind of company they are dealing with.

12. *Storytelling is memorable.* Stories are easy to remember. In fact, many stories are compelling and hard to forget.

Armstrong believes that storytelling creates an environment receptive to new ideas and change. Storytelling is a powerful force in communicating new ideas and creating change. Storytelling can help create the benefits diversity brings to organizations.

To lead us to the benefits of the diverse workforce, leaders need to develop new myths, tell new stories, and create new metaphors that will shape the future realities of their organizations.

Finding and Telling Effective Stories

Leaders need to observe the workplace and find the stories that will show diversity as beneficial. To find those stories, they must be aware of the issues and understand differences well enough to see the stories emerging. They must be good enough listeners and observers to find stories that will best create the myths to reinforce the new mission and create new ways of thinking. They need to understand rhetoric well enough to craft the stories to create the new realities of the organization.

Effective stories will show respect for people with differences, or look at people who are tolerant of others, or show people with the strength to overcome discrimination or other roadblocks to success. They will be stories that offer examples of how the organization can be, what its core values are, what its mission is.

A Core Value Story

A core value story might be, for instance, about a work group that is having problems completing a project. Traditional methods don't help them. Then, an idea from one of the group members offers a new insight, and the problems are solved, the project completed.

In this story, the group member is a man who came to this country from Thailand two years ago. The problem is in getting a piece of equipment from one area to a remote and inaccessible area. The Thai man observed a similar problem when he was selling mosquito nets to the Hill Tribes in northern Thailand as a young man. The Lisu solved the problem by putting objects on split bamboo runners. The group tried it the Lisu way, and it worked.

The story is about a Thai man using a Lisu method. It could have been about a woman, a person with a disability, or an older group member. It might have shown how traditional wisdom of some kind, an old family saying or way of doing something solved the problem. Perhaps it was a "feminine" style of looking at things that fixed what was wrong.

The story could be told in such a way to show how using differences, in both culture and experience, leads to solving problems that seem unsolvable. It could be told to show how a group was willing to try something new and unusual (to them), and how they benefited as a result. The story might show the value of utilizing each others' differences to reinforce the mission of respecting each other. Stories told from real observed examples like this will be convincing because they are authentic. A leader who communicates his or her vision persuasively can use a story, like the one created from this example, to help create that vision.

The Purpose Story

Stories can go beyond relating what a leader observes. They can relate how a leader's organization needs to evolve, and how that evolution is part of something larger than the organization. Peter Senge calls this the purpose story.[13] The larger story tells not only about where we came from and where we are going as an organization, but includes where we, as a society or as humankind, are going.

Considering the nature of embracing diversity in the workplace and its relationship to problems in our diverse society, this type of purpose story can be very powerful in an organization. Like the mission statement that strives for a larger purpose, this type of story will inspire people to work to achieve the benefits of the changes diversity brings.

Sharing the Story Organization-Wide

Leaders, then, need to listen to what is happening in their organizations, and find the emerging stories. Then, they need to tell each story in compelling and inspirational ways. The story must be framed properly, with core values and new ways of behavior emphasized, and told with the right zeal. Yet what leaders say and how they say it are only a part of leading change.

The story needs to be told to as many different audiences as possible, in as many venues as possible. It needs to be told to small groups, be included in a major address (if the leader is a high-level executive), be repeated in a variety of venues until it becomes a part of the folklore of the organization.

Telling the story enough, to enough people, and in the right way will help create the vision of the leader. It will support the organization's mission, and it will enable the organization to change so that it embraces diversity. Storytelling has been used primarily as a way of maintaining values. Storytelling can be, however, an agent of change, reinforcing new values, and creating new myths to build revitalized organizational cultures.

Diversity Tips

1. Mission statements and stories can be used to lead beneficial changes.

2. Mission statements should include, even emphasize, the diversity of the organization.

3. Getting as many people in the organization as possible to take part in the process of creating the mission statement increases their ownership in and acceptance of the mission.

4. Emerging stories can be used to influence an organization's culture and promote its leader's vision.

5. Stories can be used in ways that will create and reinforce the new values the organization needs surrounding diversity.

6. Stories should be told in as many venues as possible to make them a part of the organization's culture.

10

Leadership at Every Level

The new leader must personally engage and must somehow inspire others to do the same.

Terry Pearce[1]

After receiving an MBA from a top American business school, Hector joined a major cleaning products manufacturer and returned to his home in Buenos Aires, Argentina, to assist in a campaign for a new detergent.

The first thing he realized upon arriving home was that the manufacturer's advertising slogan and the product's scent were not right for the Argentine market. At Hector's urging, the company changed the slogan and the scent, and advertised the changes heavily. The product became the biggest success in all of South America.

While Hector was in Buenos Aires, he took three younger employees under his wing, and became their mentor and coach. All three became enormously successful and credited Hector for their achievements.

Hector's successes in Argentina led to the first of several promotions, which took him from Argentina to Brazil, from Brazil to Mexico, and from Mexico to Houston. Eventually Hector became Senior Vice President for Marketing at the corporate headquarters in Los Angeles.

REASONS FOR LEADERSHIP AT EVERY LEVEL

A company like Hector's has many leaders at every level. When people feel respected and know their input will be appreciated and potentially used, they will take on leadership roles even if they are not in leadership positions. This chapter looks at what skills executives can use to help everybody around them embrace diversity and make it work. It first looks at the need and ways to create an open environment, and then offers tools for helping assure leadership at every level in a diverse organization, including:

- Modeling
- Mentoring
- Coaching
- Reviewing Tools

AN OPEN ENVIRONMENT FOR DIVERSITY

Environment plays a big role in determining whether or not an organization can maximize the benefits of its diversity. An open environment empowers people to keep the organization moving forward. The organizational environment should be one of collaboration and support. It should be one in which everyone is encouraged to reach their potential.

The level of an executive's openness helps determine the level of an organization's openness. We explored how leaders help create organizational culture in Chapter Eight. Leaders lead by doing. How they behave sets the tone for the entire organization. The leader is only one person, though. Everyone needs to take responsibility for their organization's environment.

Taking Responsibility

Taking responsibility means taking risks. To make diversity work, as many people as possible must take responsibility. People at all levels of the organization need to teach, encourage, and help each other work towards common goals and a shared vision. An open environment supports and encourages this kind of activity.

Participative and Reflective Openness

Peter Senge, in *The Fifth Discipline,* writes about what he calls participative openness and reflective openness.[2] Participative openness lets people speak their minds. Reflective openness lets them think about what they want to say before contributing. Reflective openness requires skills of reflection and inquiry (questioning others to be sure you know what they, and you, need) It makes it safe both to speak openly and to develop skills to challenge your own and others' thinking.

Reflective openness in organizations helps make diversity work and helps develop leaders at every level. People need to feel safe enough to challenge the status quo, question how things have always been done. People who are not in leadership positions must feel it is safe for them to take risks, to intervene where they see it needed, to offer to coach someone higher than them in the organization if they have a skill the superior needs to work on. In other words, executives can help their organizations by modeling, mentoring, and coaching to develop leadership at all levels and create an organization that benefits from its diversity.

MODELING

Leaders often lead by example.

- Daw Aung San Suu Kyi, winner of the 1991 Nobel Peace Prize and leader of the Burmese democracy movement, is legendary for her ability to stand in front of guns and never show fear. Admirers follow her lead and maintain their composure as they struggle against that country's military dictatorship.

- Ben and Jerry of Ben & Jerry's Homemade, Inc. have never paid themselves exorbitantly (and created a salary structure where no manager makes an amount of money that is out of line with other employees). They also do good work in their communities. A part of their company's mission is to "improve the quality of life of a broad community: local, national, and international."[3] Ben and Jerry not only give money, but they also volunteer, go out into their communities and work with people. They encourage others in the organization to do the same.

- Lee Iacocca, former CEO of Chrysler, gave himself a one-dollar salary one year to demonstrate the need for all employees to make sacrifices and work together to rebuild the once-great automobile company.

- Consumer leader Ralph Nader lives an extremely modest lifestyle as he challenges organizations to be more responsive to the financial and other needs of the American public.

- Former President Jimmy Carter builds houses for the poor.

- Mahatma Ghandi traveled third-class on trains.

Leading by Example

Modeling good communication enables you to demonstrate both how to communicate and how to take responsibility. Former Hoechst Celanese CEO Ernest Drew saw himself as the steward of his organization's diversity initiatives. His policies—including the requirement that top officers of the company join organizations in which they were minorities—and his active support of diversity initiatives both within his company and in other community organizations are given credit for a significant turnaround, both in terms of attitudes and the bottom line.[4]

In today's organizations, people at all levels need to lead by example. Executives in particular need to model behaviors that will make diversity work. We need to learn and use the skills necessary to communicate and interact with a diverse workforce. Each of us, by modeling good behaviors, will be taking a leadership role in our organizations, no matter what our position in the organization is.

Critical Mass

The ideal is an organization where everyone treats each other with respect, where people actively listen to each other, include each other in conversations, and use each others' unique qualities to make the organization greater than the sum of its parts.

How many people is that? As in physics, just enough. Just enough to create a reaction. An organization only needs enough people behaving in such a way to reach its "critical mass."

If enough people in a diverse organization *do* learn and use good communication skills, that organization will realize the potential benefits of diversity. When enough people model good behavior, enough people will feel they are valued, enough teamwork will improve, and enough conflict will be resolved in a beneficial manner that the organization will prosper. As people see the benefits of good communication, they will try to communicate in a like manner.

Modeling Good Communication

By modeling good communication, you demonstrate both how to communicate and how to take responsibility. By knowing how to communicate well, and by doing it, others will learn from you. Your modeling will help develop new leaders, and encourage people to take leadership roles.

MENTORING

You can also specifically develop new leaders, and help others embrace diversity, by mentoring. In Greek myth, Mentor was a disguise of Athena who oversaw the education of Odysseus' son during the hero's extended absence. The word *mentor* means *counselor* or *guide.* Organizations today use the term for a person who helps in the education of another person in the organization, who guides her through the process of learning the organizational culture, and helps her learn how to be successful in her job.

At chemical giant Hoechst Celanese, for example, an African American woman engineer tells how surprised she was to realize that her white male manager understood different cultural backgrounds, including her own. He became her mentor, helping her lay out her goals as part of her career plan and working with her to reach those goals.[5]

Mentorship Programs

Some organizations officially assign mentors to new employees to help them adjust to their new environment. In others, less official mentorship programs exist. A large law firm with offices in five major cities has an unofficial system in which women partners mentor new women associates. At an electronics firm in Silicon Valley, a gay organization offers mentors for new gay employees. The aim of these types of mentorships is to help people adjust to a new environment because of their diversity and to help them do as well as they can in their organizations.

There are other types of mentoring programs to help people learn about organizations and business. At the Haas School of

Business, MBA students go out into the community with a mentorship program they created to help young people from low-income areas. They mentor them in creating small entrepreneurial businesses and in learning about the business world.

Unofficial Mentorship

Mentorship programs do not need to be official or even quasi-official. People can mentor others just by doing it. To create an open environment in which people embrace diversity, the more people who mentor others in diversity and leadership the better.

By developing your diversity communication skills, you will be in a position to teach other people your skills, and guide their development in communicating effectively in a diverse organization. By doing so, you take a leadership role and claim responsibility for making diversity work for your organization. You help people embrace diversity, and you help develop new leaders. The individuals you mentor will, in turn, potentially become mentors for others.

Mentoring: A Two-Way Street

Mentoring can occur in more than one direction. Communication skills need constant attention. We all need to work on our skills as often as possible. Communication skills in the diversity and leadership areas can be particularly difficult and are never mastered. If you know someone with great skills, latch on to her. Learn from her. Let her become your mentor. In an open environment, you can find people to mentor and help with skills, and at the same time find others whose skills you want to learn. You can find leaders at every level and can help create leaders at every level. You can help make diversity work.

Lee Iacocca knew how to use mentors. In his early years at Ford's eastern regional headquarters, he became close to his superior, Charlie Beacham, who showed him the ropes of working for that organization. When Beacham moved to Ford's corporate headquarters, he brought Iacocca along with him. Iacocca then developed a relationship with Robert McNamara. The future

Kennedy Administration Secretary of Defense helped Iacocca learn how to negotiate between competing factions at Ford, including the financial group, the product planners, factory managers, and sales executives. When McNamara became President of the Ford Motor Company in 1960, he chose Iacocca to succeed him as head of the Ford Division.

COACHING

Coaching is one of the most important skills an executive possesses. I teach coaching in my classes for MBA students, as an interpersonal skill, as part of team building, as a collaborative writing skill, and for managing diversity. 3M's Richard Lidstad states that the best style of leadership "stresses interpersonal skills . . . like listening, questioning, and getting along with others," instead of stressing command.[6] Coaching is key to developing an open environment that embraces diversity.

Motivating, Teaching, Helping

Coaching means motivating, teaching, inspiring, and helping others. It means being supportive, empathic, and open. A coach needs to be particularly adept in the art of constructive criticism (see Chapter Six). Constructive criticism motivates people and helps them by giving specific advice. Employees need to feel good about change, and about improving their performance.

Coaches in athletics are, by definition, leaders. They motivate their teams, get the most out of individuals, and facilitate people working together. Differences in coaching styles demonstrate differences in leadership styles. Tara Vanderveer, coach of the American Women's Basketball team for the 1996 Olympics, encourages her players, and shows them respect. Bobby Knight, Men's Basketball Coach at Indiana University, is a disciplinarian who coaches with a heavy hand. They both stress teamwork, though, the meaning of working together and getting the most out of each other's talents. They also both stress learning skills.

EXHIBIT 10.1
EFFECTIVE COACHING

INSTRUCTIONS: Respond to each question using the following scale:

1 = always; 2 = frequently; 3 = sometimes; 4 = seldom; 5 = never

_____ 1. Do you effectively listen to the people you are coaching?

_____ 2. Do you model the behaviors you want others to learn?

_____ 3. Do you show true concern and really care about those you coach?

_____ 4. Are you objective?

_____ 5. Do you fully explain the reasons for what you are coaching?

_____ 6. Do you give careful direction and guidance?

_____ 7. Do you keep focused on attainable goals?

_____ 8. Do you use clear, understandable language?

_____ 9. Are you honest with whomever you coach?

_____ 10. Do you stretch people's talents?

_____ 11. Are you enthusiastic and positive?

_____ 12. Do you communicate pride in the people you have coached?

SCORING: Add up your numbers. The closer to 12 you are, the more effective you are as a coach.

Knowing Diversity and Communication Skills

From the beginning of this book, I have said that we have to know how to communicate in a diverse organization in order to be effective executives. We need to know the skills in order to teach them and motivate others to use them. We need to understand the skills well enough to spot people who need help with them, to understand what they are missing, and be able to help them with their deficiencies.

Coaching Each Other

Coaching is not only a manager's job. We can all coach each other and teach each other skills. If we have helped create an open environment in our organization, it doesn't matter what position the person has in the organization. In an open environment, everyone can coach each other. I might coach you on one skill, you might coach me on another. By coaching each other, we each get better, and the organization thrives.

One of the best teams I have ever been involved with was my team of Graduate Student Instructors my first year at Berkeley. Almost every one of the seven members was a superior coach. We all coached each other all the time. Even though I was the "teacher," I was constantly learning. Every individual learned, and the team grew into a superior unit, the highest rated group of GSIs in the program.

Coaching Diversity and Leadership Skills

Coaching diversity skills is difficult. Understanding differences is not easy, and all of us have biases that we need to deal with. One of the skills we teach in coaching diversity skills is patience, and we need patience to coach these skills.

Coaching leadership is also difficult. Some say leadership is something that cannot be taught. You can, however, coach someone on the skills required for leadership. You can encourage someone to take on a leadership role. This might mean intervening if she sees discrimination. It might mean having the courage to speak to her supervisor about a stereotype she sees her supervisor perpetuating. It might mean modeling good skills and mentoring and coaching others.

Leadership at Every Level

As I have stated previously, the more people take on leadership roles, the fewer problems there will be with diversity, the more benefits reaped. A person who takes on a leadership role in diversity, who understands diversity and can communicate with a diverse workforce, and who can facilitate production from a diverse workforce, is the best-equipped manager and leader. Executives help everyone in the organization by encouraging leadership at every level.

Diversity Skills: A Continuous Process

In order to model, mentor, and coach, we need to continually work on our skills. That is especially true when these skills are practiced in a diverse workplace.

Understanding diversity and realizing its benefits in the workplace is, like any dynamic phenomenon, an ongoing process. The keys to benefiting from diversity are self-awareness and understanding. No one "gets" diversity any more than one simply achieves self-awareness and understanding and then goes on to something else. They are life processes. We must continue to work on self-awareness, on understanding differences. Diversity means differences; and as long as there are differences, we must be prepared for the unexpected, ready to anticipate the new twist, and to watch out for the potential misunderstanding. That means taking responsibility for not assuming that what is not immediately known is not knowable.

Part of taking responsibility means being sure that you understand communication, understand how to take a leadership role in your organization, and understand how to help others do the same. Following are key points, the tools you need in the diverse environment, followed by a self-assessment that you can use to track your own development:

- **Self-Awareness Skills:** understand your own background; become more conscious of your values; recognize and challenge the perceptions, assumptions, and biases that affect your thinking; recognize your areas of insecurity and how they may affect your communication; examine your communication style; ask for feedback on how clearly you communicate; ask other questions about yourself, and listen to the answers; roll the D.I.E.; and continually work on your self-awareness.

- **Listening:** frequently check the accuracy of your perceptions; use paraphrasing and summarizing; work on reducing obstacles to effective listening; listen to learn about others.

- **Empathy:** actively attempt to see things from another person's point of view; think about times you have been a member of a nondominant group, and how you felt; respect and appreciate differences in communication style, background, and values.

- **Nonverbal Communication:** remember that gestures and other body language, preferences for distance, and conceptions of time vary among cultural groups; watch for indications that someone is confused or embarrassed; be sure you understand the nonverbal communication before you respond.

- **Understanding Different Communication Styles:** understand the general nature of different styles of communication; if you are having a problem with a particular group, learn all you can about that group; learn what you can about communication and culture; learn about your own and other groups' experience, history, culture.

- **Effective Communication Skills:** be open; listen proactively; communicate empathy; use inclusive language; speak with a sense of equality; be supportive; exhibit confidence; be other-oriented; be flexible; metacommunicate.

- **Leadership Skills:** take responsibility; empower others to take leadership roles; find the emerging stories and tell them in a way that builds understanding; become skilled in delivering constructive criticism; develop problem-solving skills, conflict management skills, and mediation skills; understand and use rhetoric.

FINAL SELF-ASSESSMENT

As a last thing to do before closing the covers of this book, here is a final self-assessment. Again, you will always need to work on these skills. Test yourself every now and then to see how you are doing, and find which skills need the most work at that time. This relatively short assessment is intended to help you think about issues in a slightly different way. It is another tool to hone your skills so you will be able to model, mentor, and coach to create leadership at every level.

EXHIBIT 10.2
SELF-ASSESSMENT

General:

☐ Am I well informed about my organization's philosophy and policies on diversity issues?

☐ Do I observe my own communication to avoid sexist, racist, or other intolerant behaviors?

☐ Do I tend to defer to and accommodate others in group settings?

☐ Do I avoid favoring the members of one gender or other group by responding more frequently or positively?

☐ Do I avoid rewarding dominating behavior more than collaborating or supporting behavior?

☐ As a facilitator, am I creative about using group processes that encourage even participation from members of all groups?

Nonverbal

☐ Do I observe how women and men physically arrange themselves in a room (e.g., the seating arrangement)?

☐ Do I notice when people try to influence a meeting by standing instead of sitting, taking up additional space (e.g., by draping an arm or leg over another chair or desk)?

☐ Do I pay more attention to one group than to the other (standing with, facing, directing more eye contact to, nodding at, smiling at, etc.)?

(Continued)

EXHIBIT 10.2
SELF-ASSESSMENT *(Concluded)*

Verbal

☐ Do I pay attention to the amount of time I speak compared with others in group settings?

☐ Do I frequently interrupt others?

☐ Do I avoid the use of stereotypes?

☐ Do I exclude people with my language?

☐ Do I make joking or slighting remarks at the expense of one group?

☐ Do I confront inappropriate sexist, racist, homophobic, or ageist comments or behaviors by others?

☐ Do I tend to give longer, more complete responses to one group than to another?

☐ Do I solicit more contributions from one group than from another?

☐ Do I de-emphasize or ignore the contributions from one group more than another?

☐ Do I find fault with people who behave in counter-stereotypical ways?

Diversity Tips

1. Take responsibility in creating an open environment in your organization.

2. Know the communication skills you need to be an effective communicator in a diverse organization.

3. Model your good communication skills.

4. Mentor people whose diversity and communication skills need improvement.

5. Find a mentor who can help you improve your skills.

6. Coach others on how to be good communicators and take responsibility in making diversity work.

7. Continually work on and review your diversity, leadership, and communication skills.

Notes

CHAPTER 1

1. Peter Senge, *The Fifth Discipline* (New York: Doubleday, 1990).
2. David Tuller, "True Colors," *San Francisco Chronicle*, Mar. 3, 1996.
3. Richard Lidstad, "The Qualities of Success," *Vital Speeches of the Day* (June 1995): 559–61.
4. Faye Rice, "How to Make Diversity Pay," *Fortune*, Aug. 8, 1994: 78–86.
5. Senge, *The Fifth Discipline*; also in Senge, "The Leader's New Work: Building Learning Organizations," *Sloan Management Review* (Fall, 1970).
6. Kenneth Burke, *Language as Symbolic Action* (Berkeley: University of California Press, 1973).

CHAPTER 2

1. *San Francisco Chronicle*, Mar. 3, 1996.
2. Michelle Galen, "Beyond the Numbers Game," *Businessweek*, Aug. 14, 1995: 60–61.
3. Ronni Sandroff, "Sexual Harassment in the Fortune 500," *Working Woman* (December 1988).
4. Linda Stamato, "Sexual Harassment in the Workplace: Is Mediation an Appropriate Forum?" *New Jersey Law Journal* (Aug. 15, 1994): 16.
5. David Tuller, "True Colors," *San Francisco Chronicle*, Mar. 3, 1996.
6. Kathleen Pender, "Management Lacks Women," *San Francisco Chronicle*, January 18, 1996.

CHAPTER 3

1. Adapted from Marquita Byrd, *The Intracultural Communication Book* (1993).
2. Milton Rokeach, *Beliefs, Attitudes, and Values* (San Francisco: Jossey-Bass, 1968) and *The Nature of Human Values* (New York: Free Press, 1973).

3. Faye Rice, "How to Make Diversity Pay," *Fortune,* Aug. 8, 1994: 78–86.

CHAPTER 4

1. Sam Keen, *Fire in the Belly* (New York: Bantam Books, 1991).
2. Faye Rice, "How to Make Diversity Pay," *Fortune,* Aug. 8, 1994: 78–86.
3. Michelle Galen, "Beyond the Numbers Game," *Businessweek,* Aug. 14, 1995: 60–61.
4. Lee Gardenschwartz and Anita Rowe, *The Diversity Tool Kit* (New York: Irwin Professional Publishing, 1993).
5. Lee Gardenschwartz and Anita Rowe, *Managing Diversity* (New York: Irwin Professional Publishing, 1993).
6. Deborah Tannen, *You Just Don't Understand: Men and Women in Conversation* (New York: William Morrow and Company, 1990).
7. Adapted from Julia T. Wood, "Gender, Communication, and Culture," in Larry Samovar and Richard Porter, *Intercultural Communication: A Reader,* 7th ed. (New York: Wadsworth, 1994), pp. 155–64.

CHAPTER 5

1. Max DePree, *Leadership Is an Art* (New York: Dell Publishing, 1989), p. 9.
2. From the University of Maryland Policy on Inclusive Language.
3. Adapted from TARGET ACCESS (San Jose State University of Recreation and Leisure Studies); SJSU Students with Disabilities; Hearing Society for the Bay Area; National Easter Seals Society; and the staff of SJSU Disabled Students Office.
4. Michelle Galen, "Beyond the Numbers Game," *Businessweek,* Aug. 14, 1995: 60–61.
5. From David Whetten and Kim Cameron, *Developing Management Skills: Communicating Supportively* (New York: HarperCollins, 1993), p. 33.

CHAPTER 6

1. Michael Ray and Alan Rinzler, eds., *The New Paradigm in Business* (Los Angeles: Jeremy Tarcher/Perigee, 1993), p. 64.
2. Cassandra Hayes, "The New Spin on Corporate Work Teams," *Black Enterprise* (June 1995): 229–30+.
3. Hayes, p. 230.
4. Gardenschwartz and Rowe, *Managing Diversity.*

Chapter 7

1. Roger Fisher and Scott Brown, *Getting Together: Building Relationships as We Negotiate* (New York: Penguin, 1989), p. 85.
2. *Webster's Encyclopedic Unabridged Dictionary of the English Language,* 1989.
3. Ronni Sandroff, "Sexual Harassment in the Fortune 500," *Working Woman* (December 1988).
4. Linda Stamato, "Sexual Harassment in the Workplace: Is Mediation an Appropriate Forum?" *New Jersey Law Journal* (Aug. 15, 1994): 16.
5. Dean Barnlund, Lectures, 1975–78.
6. Adapted from Joseph A. DeVito, *The Interpersonal Communication Book* (New York: HarperCollins, 1992).
7. Adapted from Thomas Ruble and Kenneth Thomas, "Support for a Two-dimensional Model of Conflict Behavior," *Organizational Behavior and Human Performance* 16 (1976): 145.
8. I have seen many metaphors over the years. I adapted these from the unpublished writing of Karen Lovaas, but I am unsure of their origin.
9. Michael Doyle and David Strauss, *How to Make Meetings Work* (New York: Jove Books, 1982).
10. Sharon Nelton, "Nurturing Diversity," *Nation's Business,* June 1995: 25–27.
11. From Dean Whetten and Kim Cameron, *Developing Management Skills*; and adapted from W. Morris and S. Saskin, *Organizational Behavior in Action* (St. Paul: West Publishing, 1976).
12. Warren Bennis, "Learning Some Basic Truisms about Leadership," in Michael Ray and Alan Rinzler, eds. *The New Paradigm in Business* (Los Angeles: Jeremy Tarcher/Perigee, 1993), p. 76.

Chapter 8

1. James C. Collins and Jerry Porras, "Purpose, Mission, and Vision," in Ray and Rinzler, *The New Paradigm in Business,* p. 88.
2. R. Tunley, "Mary Kay's Sweet Smell of Success," *Reader's Digest,* Nov. 1978.
3. Kenneth Burke, *Rhetoric of Motives* (Berkeley: University of California Press, 1974), p. 43.
4. Terry Pearce, *Leading Out Loud* (San Francisco: Jossey-Bass, 1995), p.61.
5. Kenneth Burke, *Language as Symbolic Action* (Berkeley: University of California Press, 1973).

6. Burke, *Rhetoric of Motives,* p. 40–42.
7. Pearce, *Leading Out Loud,* p. 93
8. Tarah M. Walters, "Successfully Managing Diversity," *Vital Speeches of the Day* (June 1, 1995): 496–500.
9. Pearce, *Leading Out Loud,* pp. 107–110.
10. Barry Eckhouse, *Competitive Communication* (New York: McGraw-Hill, 1994), p. 59.

CHAPTER 9

1. Ray and Rinzler, *The New Paradigm in Business,* p. 226.
2. James C. Collins and Jerry Porras, *Built to Last: Successful Habits of Visionary Companies* (New York: HarperCollins, 1994).
3. Peter Senge, "The Leader's New Work: Building Learning Organizations," *Sloan Management Review* (Fall 1970): 9.
4. Senge, p. 10.
5. Bobbi Nodell, "All Eyes on the Prize," *Oakland Tribune,* October 2, 1995.
6. Jeffrey Abrahams, *The Mission Statement Book* (Berkeley: Ten Speed Press, 1995), p. 370.
7. Abrahams, p. 49.
8. Nodell.
9. Jay Conger, *The Charismatic Leader* (San Francisco: Jossey-Bass, 1989).
10. Conger.
11. David Armstrong, *Managing by Storying Around* (New York: Doubleday, 1992).
12. Armstrong.
13. Senge, *The Fifth Discipline,* p. 354.

CHAPTER 10

1. Terry Pearce, *Leading Out Loud* (San Francisco: Jossey-Bass, 1995), p. 13
2. Peter Senge, *The Fifth Discipline: The Art and Practice of the Learning Organization* (New York: Doubleday, 1990).
3. Jeffrey Abrahams, *The Mission Statement Book* (Berkeley: Ten Speed Press, 1995), p. 125.
4. Faye Rice, "How to Make Diversity Pay," *Fortune,* Aug. 8, 1994: 78–86.
5. Rice, p. 80.
6. Richard Lidstad, "The Qualities of Success," *Vital Speeches of the Day* (June 1995): 559–61.

Selected Readings

Abrahams, Jeffrey. The *Mission Statement Book*. Berkeley: Ten Speed Press, 1995.

Armstrong, David M. *Managing By Storying Around*. New York: Doubleday Currency, 1992.

Burke, Kenneth. *Rhetoric of Motives*. Berkeley: University of California Press, 1974.

———. *Language As Symbolic Action*. Berkeley: University of California Press, 1973.

Chesebro, James W., ed. *Gayspeak: Gay Male & Lesbian Communications*. New York: Pilgrim Press, 1981.

Doyle, Michael and David Straus, *How To Make Meetings Work*. New York: Jove Books, 1982.

Eckhouse, Barry. *Competitive Communication,* 2nd ed. New York: McGraw-Hill, Inc., 1994.

Gardenschwartz, Lee and Anita Rowe. *Managing Diversity*. New York: Irwin Professional Publishing, 1993.

Pearce, Terry. *Leading Out Loud*. San Francisco: Jossey-Bass Publishers, 1995.

Ray, Michael and Alan Rinzler, Eds., *The New Paradigm in Business*. Los Angeles: Jeremy Tarcher/Perigee, 1993.

Samovar, Larry A. and Richard E. Porter, eds. *Intercultural Communication: A Reader,* 7th ed. New York: Wadsworth, 1994.

Senge, Peter, *The Fifth Discipline*. New York: Doubleday/Currency, 1990.

Tannen, Deborah. *Talking From 9 to 5*. New York: William Morrow and Company, Inc., 1994.

———. *You Just Don't Understand: Women and Men in Conversation*. New York: William Morrow and Company, Inc., 1990.

Van Nostrand, Catherine Herr. *Gender-Responsible Leadership*. Newbury Park, CA: Sage, 1993.

West, Cornell. *Race Matters*. Boston: Beacon Press, 1993.

Index

About the Author

For more than twenty years William Sonnenschein has been a communications consultant, teacher and manager. He is principal of his own consulting practice, based in Oakland, California. The consultancy develops communications curricula and training programs and conducts workshops and courses for business and industry. He also consults in such current communications issues as diversity cross-gender communication, leadership, and conflict management.

His clients include Hewlett-Packard, Chevron, Mervyn's Department Stores, and numerous government and nonprofit organizations. Sonnenschein is a member of the Communications Group Faculty at the Haas School of Business, University of California, Berkeley.

TITLES OF INTEREST IN
BUSINESS AND INTERNATIONAL BUSINESS

GLOBAL MARKETING IMPERATIVE, by Michael Czinkota, Ilkka Ronkainen, and John Tarrant
MARKETING STRATEGIES FOR GROWTH IN UNCERTAIN TIMES, by Allan J. Magraph
INNOVATION: LEADERSHIP STRATEGIES FOR THE COMPETITIVE EDGE, by Thomas D. Kuczmanski
INTERACTIVE MARKETING: THE FUTURE PRESENT, by Edward Forrest and Richard Mizerski
THE SUCCESSFUL MARKETING PLAN, by Roman Hiebing and Scott Cooper
STRATEGIC DATABASE MARKETING, by Rob Jackson and Paul Wang
CUSTOMER BONDING, by Richard Cross and Janet Smith
MANAGING SALES LEADS by Bob Donath, Richard A. Crocker, Carol K. Dixon,
     and James W. Obermayer
AMA MARKETING ENCYCLOPEDIA, by Jeffrey Heilbrun
BETWEEN CULTURES, by H. Ned Seelye and Jacqueline Howell Wasilewski
HOW TO CREATE HIGH-IMPACT BUSINESS PRESENTATIONS, by Joyce Kupsh and Pat Graves
EFFECTIVE BUSINESS DECISION MAKING, by William F. O'Dell
HOW TO GET PEOPLE TO DO THINGS YOUR WAY, by J. Robert Parkinson
HANDBOOK FOR MEMO WRITING, by L. Sue Baugh
HANDBOOK FOR BUSINESS WRITING, by L. Sue Baugh, Maridell Fryar, and David A. Thomas
HANDBOOK FOR PROOFREADING, by Laura Killen Anderson
HANDBOOK FOR TECHNICAL WRITING, James Shelton
HOW TO BE AN EFFECTIVE SPEAKER, by Christina Stuart
FORMAL MEETINGS, by Alice N. Pohl
COMMITTEES AND BOARDS, by Alice N. Pohl
MEETINGS: RULES AND PROCEDURES, by Alice N. Pohl
BIG MEETINGS, BIG RESULTS, by Tom McMahon
HOW TO GET THE MOST OUT OF TRADE SHOWS, by Steve Miller
HOW TO GET THE MOST OUT OF SALES MEETINGS, by James Dance
A BASIC GUIDE TO EXPORTING, by U.S. Department of Commerce
A BASIC GUIDE TO IMPORTING, by U.S. Customs Service
CULTURE CLASH, by Ned Seelye and Alan Seelye-James
DOING BUSINESS IN RUSSIA by ALM Consulting, Frere Chomeley Bischoff;
     and KPMG Peat Marwick
THE INTERNATIONAL BUSINESS BOOK, by Vincent Guy and John Matlock
INTERNATIONAL BUSINESS CULTURE SERIES, by Peggy Kenna and Sondra Lacy
INTERNATIONAL HERALD TRIBUNE: DOING BUSINESS IN TODAY'S WESTERN EUROPE by Alan Tillier
INTERNATIONAL HERALD TRIBUNE: GUIDE TO EUROPE, by Alan Tillier and Roger Beardwood
INTERNATIONAL HERALD TRIBUNE: GUIDE TO BUSINESS TRAVEL IN ASIA, by Robert K. McCabe
DOING BUSINESS WITH CHINA
MARKETING TO CHINA, by Xu Bai-Yi
THE JAPANESE INFLUENCE ON AMERICA, by Boye De Mente
JAPANESE ETIQUETTE & ETHICS IN BUSINESS, by Boye De Mente
CHINESE ETIQUETTE & ETHICS IN BUSINESS, by Boye De Mente
KOREAN ETIQUETTE & ETHICS IN BUSINESS, by Boye De Mente

For further information or a current catalog, write:
NTC Business Books
a division of NTC *Publishing Group*
4255 West Touhy Avenue
Lincolnwood, Illinois 60646–1975